TREEHOUSE

TREEHOUSE

NEW AND SELECTED POEMS

WILLIAM KLOEFKORN

WHITE PINE PRESS · FREDONIA, NEW YORK

Publication of this book was made possible, in part, by grants from the National Endowment for the Arts and the New York State Council on the Arts.

Ackowledgments:
Some of these poems have previously appeared in the following magazines: *North Dakota Quarterly, Poet & Critic, Laurel Review, Midwest Quarterly, Zone 3, Midwest Poetry Review, South Dakota Review, Tar River Poetry,* and *Leaves of Grass.*

Cover Drawing: Gregory J. Hartel

Book Design: Elaine LaMattina

Printed and Bound in the United States of America.

ISBN 1-877727-65-2

First Edition

1 3 5 7 9 10 8 6 4 2

Published by
      White Pine Press
      10 Village Square
      Fredonia, New York 14063

—to the memory of my father,
Ralph

CONTENTS

NEW POEMS

FROM *LET THE DANCE BEGIN*

TREEHOUSE

Not Dreaming

—at a football game, early fall

Don't tell me that this grandstand
isn't a solid disguise
for the ship that will take me away
from what must surely be illusory.

To see figures in gold and black,
with their bumps and grinds—
they are far too much of what they are
to be believed in. Already

beneath me the hull of this massive bark
heaves heavily to what I'm
told is starboard. And those other
bodies beyond the bumps and grinds—

don't tell me they are anything more than hulks
brilliant and anonymous
adrift on their way to drowning. And
don't tell me that always

there isn't another place arcadian
to be rowed to,
fronds and pistachios
and natives lining the shore,

their faces without speaking
saying Go away, saying
Welcome. Don't tell me
they are figments

of a windjammer's imagination. If so,
why is this grandstand
heaving heavily to starboard? And why am I
here, on this field of green and of fury,

beside you, not dreaming?

That Summer

That summer between high school
and what turned out to be
a lingering college education

I worked as a gandy-dancer
on the railroad, Panhandle Division
of the AT&SF, and the Oklahoma sun

turned my skin brown as a berry,
my arms and hands especially,
so that when I worked at foreplay

in the back seat of my old Bel-Air
my large dark hands
against her milk-white breasts

made me think of Sunday-school,
of how Jesus, we were told, loves equally
his children—red and yellow,

black and white—and I'd hum the tune
that went with the words,
and she'd hum with me,

above us the domelight shining
because I had turned it on
to exploit the contrast,

as if contrast matters, which it does,
our differences moving us into each other
as the earth, so apparently inert,

so swiftly moves.

Rope

Or maybe it's not a rope, after all,
but instead an obese snake
you trip across while
snitching snowpeas from your keeper's
garden. With a V-headed stick
say you pin the bullsnake
to the well-mulched earth
to decapitate it with the thick blade
on your Barlow. Dragging the long limp body
then behind, you run it
as if a severed shirtsleeve with its arm intact
through the Maytag's wringers,
transforming it from snake to the strop
your keeper turns you a funny shade of blue
with. Not that you don't deserve it:
thief and despoiler of machines,
certainly in this best of all possible schemes
you have it coming. So you
bite your lip, you don't cry out,
you take it, knowing beyond
somebody else's book of justice
what you know:

in the haymow the rope
you happened upon just yesterday
lies coiled, its noose
as if the mouth of a confidante
impatient to teach someone who's never too old,
they say, to learn
a lesson.

Rancher

One early afternoon a man
from Wichita, a slicker,
walked into my father's narrow restaurant,
and before his hot-beef sandwich
disappeared from its platter
he had convinced my father to become
what four weeks later
he tried his level best to begin to be:
a rancher.

Between Kiowa and Medicine Lodge
we settled in,
father with his floating kidney, his
double hernia,
mother with ample hands still
smelling of French fries from the café,
brother and sister as if mostly eyes,
four porcelain saucers
each with a perfect blueness
at its center.

In this snapshot that's my pitiful brother
lugging water to pacify the bull.
What isn't in the picture is me
hiding behind the woodstack
to watch that bull
with its fencepost of a cock
service the heifer.

In the haymow at night, all exits secured,
I one by one

destroyed the swallows,
my brother with a flashlight
holding them blinded
on a beam along the barn's eternal ribs,
the rafters.

When the milkcow managed
to outwit her hobble
guess who in spite of a double hernia
beat that cow almost to death
with a milkstool?

My father.

In this one I'm sitting bareback
on my favorite pony, a roan,
whose name I cannot remember.
I'm about to ride off
to count the newborn calves.
Not in the picture is my little brother,
who crying from his place
beside the milkhouse
calls me an unkind name, says
You're not old enough,
either.

Each month my father wrote a check,
mailed it then to the Wichita slicker.
What I knew was not only what I sensed,
but what I saw:
father's truss like a lonely tangle of harness
hanging from a nail just
inside the bedroom

door.
My sister: a brace of porcelain eyes
each with a distant blueness
at its center.

My mother.

And in this one, as you can see,
it's all over. On the way back
to that home we had moved away from
we stopped for carry-out hamburgers.
That's me beside the heaped-up trailer,
about to take my first dislocated bite.
What isn't in the picture:
the front half of the car, or
my sister beside my mother in the front seat, or
father about to settle behind the wheel, or
what happened when we hit the road
again to home, or
what might yet happen should in fact
we get there.

Separations

We'll see,
mother says,
meaning probably not,

meaning that the cowboy outfit
will either remain forever
on the catalog's slick page

or maybe what is worse
ride off into the sunset
on the body of the boy

whose mother said yes.
We'll see, mother says,
and I join her at the window

to watch my father
with his pitiful knapsack
become a flyspeck

at the center of the narrow
gravel road. Already
I am a full head taller

than my mother. Before long
I'll have a date, my first
with someone mother

will strongly disapprove of.
We'll see, she says,
her large eyes vacant

in the glass we strain to look
through, but
even as the words are spoken

the diminutive that was
my father
drops out of sight.

Sycamore

Always it's the tree Zacchaeus climbed
to see the Master, to hear him say at last
*Zacchaeus, come down from there! I'm going
to your house for tea.*

Always the bark rough as pre-
diluvian skin,
always each fallen leaf large as the map
of a hemisphere.

And I imagine Zacchaeus, that gutsy loner,
so nervous in his tiny kitchen he spills the tea,
imagine then the Master from a distance
wiping clean the linoleum—Look, Mom,
no hands!

Back home in Kansas meanwhile
it's the cottonwood
aslant at a most precarious angle
over the sun-rippled current of Sand Creek
I climb,

naked almost as the jay that squawks
above me. This time, I tell myself,
I'll raise my arms just so
to do the dive, this time,
precisely right, knowing
what I know: I am now,
and have always been,

alive. My faith therefore is this,
that the myth is the fact's obtuse reflection—
always the flesh free-falling,
always the house sufficient to take it in.

Waitress

She's the one from my long-neglected
Trilogy of the Lost
I most remember,

the one whose face, given
half a chance,
might sour milk,

and I confess that at first glance
I covered my cup
with my left hand

until the steam
became too much
for skin to bear—and

when I raised the hand
how the steam
obscured to dignify the face:

that, and what I
came to realize morning
into morning: white teeth

of her crooked smile,
swift motion
of a milk-white apron, fist

pale with its vessel of drug
like the warm dependency
I dream of

always there. Until
one morning it wasn't,
in its place what I had nothing

better to do than to notice,
myself in a mirror
behind a shelf of tobacco

and blades and candy,
between us nothing to obscure us
into dignity, half of us gone

to God knows where, that other half
deep in a field
of way leading on to way,

and every now and then, at its oddest
hour, unable
not to remember.

Cures

With her right index finger
mother probes the jar,
brings forth a dollop of Vicks,
panacea she forces deep into my throat,
and gagging I lie back down
to breathe my mother's cure
into sheet and quiltblock
until cough gives way
to silence so total
it must be sleep.

Where the skin of my left
thigh used to be
she tenders Cloverine salve,
Denver Mud six months from now
when I test the fire too closely,
poultice and woodstove as if
that marriage made anywhere
except in Heaven. But for the moment
it's Cloverine—and
if I sell the entire case
the Red Ryder BB gun will be mine.

Old Mrs. Cozad across the street
buys me out,
and watching her move
like a tall delicate animal
to the table to rummage her purse
I wonder if there is any spot
on the warp or the woof of her body
not wanting cured.

When at last the gun arrives
I cannot wait
to squeeze the trigger
to wound the dove,
large bird flapping what life it has left
onto the old woman's front porch,
dry unpainted pine
frantic with blooddrops. Is the sun
playing games,
or is that the old woman's face
depleted at the window?

When Mrs. Cozad dies
mother in spite of herself
laughs to learn that
I care.
Don't cry, she says,
always it could be worse—
leaving me to learn the cure
day by day, year by year,
youngster at the door at startling intervals
bright-faced to sell that ointment
too expedient if not too rich
for human tears.

The Day the Earthquake
Was Scheduled to Happen But Didn't

I'm out in the back yard
filling the bird feeder,
looking off in the general direction

of the Missouri boondocks, where
the earthquake was scheduled to happen
but didn't,

when all at once a voice like a tremor
unsettles my ear, saying how
if I intend to have the sidewalks

shoveled clean before nightfall
I'd better stop dawdling,
I'd better remove the lead

from wherever I have it stashed
and shift my archaic frame
into a more productive gear,

so insofar as my constitution allows
I do just that,
but scoop as I may

I can't out-scoop the sundown,
meaning that I'm still rearranging snow
when a quarter-moon shows itself

glorious and albino
atop the horizon. So I take a break,
lean on the handle of the shovel

like a common laborer,
watch the moon in its rising
become a portable nest

for all those birds I hope one day
to be a part of
somehow among the branches

of the steadfast linden.

Monday Morning

I enter my office to confirm what just outside,
standing in the hallway,
fumbling a key into an early-morning lock,

I suspected: the cleaning lady already has done
her work, has taken her
massive body into the room to rearrange the dust,

with her sweat and her massive mop to leave
a day-long wake of dank
effluvium. She is that monumental irony

out of Dickens who soils by cleaning. Yet I cannot
forget that day when,
having worked overtime to despoil the room,

she collapsed in the widest chair to tell me more
than I cared to hear
of her misbegotten daughter. Opening windows, I

listened: the abuses, the lopsided child, the jerk
who can never hold a job,
and so on. I can no more forget than honestly

believe her. Yet when at last she rises, lifting
slowly the sloshy burden
of her paraphernalia, I help her into the hallway,

her eyes from the vaults of their soft and massive face
dropping tears the size
of marbles onto an oak floor tragically in need

of reconstruction. Soon then within a cloud of exudation
I find the text I'll be
talking about in class: long ago and far away—

and yet somehow immediate to the very core—the woman
who killed her sons
for spite, the man who would be king.

In Switzerland

In Switzerland
my brother pulls over
at the top of a rise

overlooking the postcard
I'll buy tonight to
send back home—

and as he relieves himself
I yodel,
my falsettos distinct and

redundant, convincing
to the point that my brother
relaxed now behind the wheel

says so,
his compliment rare as this
early-morning atmosphere

we drive through
on our way to the Old Country,
to the wide old woman

in the Gasthaus who if
she wasn't drinking beer
would be our grandmother,

on then to the little cemetery
where sure enough
we'll find those names

we so often heard her speak of,
our own among them—
Johann, Wilhelm—

my brother driving probably
faster than he should
as though if he missed a curve

our missing would be little more
than sound against the incline
of an earthen wall,

an echo.

Non-Stop Begonias

Each morning I sit for one hour
in the sanctity of my back yard,
sipping black coffee and

studying the non-stop begonias.
That's what they're called, all right,
their large thin petals of white and pink

blooming non-stop as if the oriental blades
of some fair maidens' fans. It's
not a bad life, this

early-morning hour of concentration,
though yesterday when the clouds rolled in
I almost yielded,

raindrops more plentiful than moments
pelting the skin. But I stayed on. I
could sense a modicum of their secret

escaping into the dense electric air
from them to me,
and when the clouds gave way to blue

I stood full-length
without benefit of crutch or cane,
without crutch or cane I walked then

non-stop into any and everything it took
to bring me back to where
I am this morning.

Returning

This morning in the *Star*
I read that the woman who
survived the beating and the rape

and the bottomless fall from the bridge
returned to the scene
seventeen years later,

husband and child with her,
this time to do the pushing herself,
her body carried away this time

in a torrent of noncommittal river.
And because the mind
refuses to be the good dog

rolling over,
I try to single out that moment
among all those others most abysmal,

to pin it down to be in spite of premonition
somehow returned to.
It's the touchstone that sharpens

not only itself but everything else,
not excluding the joyous.
This morning, for example,

having stooped to lift the paper
from the front porch
I looked up to see stars in the west

giving way to an impending sunrise.
Standing between sunrise and star
I knew for an instant the thrill

of one swift life giving way to another.
I was going under for the third time,
according to mother,

her account so vivid I both see and
believe it. The air I breathed at last
was immensely sweet,

and because I could not breathe it
deeply enough
I swallowed and swallowed it,

its taste on my tongue
long into the evening
as lying on my back on a cot

beneath our Chinese elm
I saw among the limbs and the leaves
this star, that star, another

into another star, returning.

Drums

> If no one remembered to bring a drum, we
> used the top of a Volkswagen.
>
> —*Laura Tohe*

Even as a small boy I knew this much:
every pow-wow needs a drum.

And because my own frail life was itself
a daily preparation for some grand ceremony
to be conducted some grand day
somewhere
I convinced my mother that if she'd buy me
Jimmy Ridgway's snare
I'd die before I asked of her
another single solitary thing.

It was a beauty, its taut skin
bright with the handiwork of stencils—
Popeye, Smilin' Jack, Andy Gump,

the Katzenjammer Kids, Jiggs.
Under an elm at dusk
I practiced those goofy figures
slowly into oblivion. And when Jimmy Ridgway,
who couldn't wait to rectify Pearl Harbor,
returned,

it was his father who couldn't bring himself
to leave the gravesite,
his thick bricklayer's fingers
thumping a soft Morse code

into the rich and enduring mahogany
of coffin.

Tonight, driving home, I hear a downpour
doing its flims and flams
on the roof of my Skylark,
and with white knuckles
I beat my own tattoo against the steering wheel.
I have been away just long enough to know
that even the straight road
sooner or later
circles,

this earth the head of a sacred drum
we listen to
to catch if not fully understand
its sound.

First Night of a Weekend
Fishing With My Brother

Long after sundown
we stand at the backyard plank
filleting crappie and catfish,
trusting chiefly to touch until the moon
rises high enough to give us light,
then burying the spines with heads attached
we shower under barrels
of sun-warmed water, our flesh
white as the bellies of those
channels we had lifted
flopping and sleek into the jonboat.

We sit on campstools at the edge
of the lake,
drinking our tin cups dry,
watching the face of a full moon
work its quaint contortions
on a surface of breeze-blown water.
So little to do, my brother says,
and so much time in which
to do it.

So we do it,
together seeing first the moon
abandon the water, next the stars
move out to let the thunderheads in,
until beside a fire we watch a steady rain
confront the flames,
my brother cheering the moisture,
my own sympathies inclined

toward the heat
I later move my body into,
tent and sleeping bag and breath,
time as if liquid and pervasive
filling each otherwise
empty vessel to over-
flowing.

Stealing Melons

I'm with my buddy Ray stealing melons
when suddenly the night
explodes,
and we know old man McClung well enough
to believe he'll not point that shotgun
deliberately our way,
but because we are trespassing, after all,
we can't be absolutely certain,
so we hug the ground,
waiting for time to do what time's
created for—to take care of things,
to smooth things over.

What I know most clearly is what
I can most cleanly inhale—
old man McClung's damp sandy earth,
beside me my buddy Ray in soft spasms
giggling,
as if danger were a joke with a distant
and corny punchline, a huge shaggy dog
he'd risk his life to rise
to scratch behind the ears of.

Which
more or less he does,
ignoring my admonition—Stay down!—
to become fully erect at that moment
when a full watermelon moon   ·
outshines the clouds. And what
I know least clearly is what
I most hazily foresee—my buddy Ray two weeks from now

smashing our high school's rushing record,
and doing it
against those big-time pricks from Plainview,
that blood on his Bulldog jersey
coming from his own bloodstream through which
two years from now
white-shirted blockers will be too few
to keep him scrambling.

When the night for a second time
explodes
my buddy Ray moans quietly, with both hands
clutches his abdomen, with a grimace
drops like a stone
beside the oblong torso of a melon. Of course
I go directly to the deed that
must be done:
with the long blade of my Barlow
I halve the melon, from each half
disengage the heart. With my buddy Ray
I sit in Kansas moonlight then
grinning white teeth into red forbidden fruit,
time meanwhile doing surely
what it's made to do: move forever
standing always still.

Walking Home, Late October

Because my *Agamemnon* is falling apart
I welcome the blue rubberband
lying among a scattering of others,
surplus no doubt from the paperboy's
long afternoon of rolling and of binding.
I pick it up, stretch it around the text,

continue homeward. What I notice
mostly are the trees, mostly the bur oak,
the linden, the sycamore. And maybe because
I went to the bar instead of directly home,
I think of that ancient woman, Clytaemestra,
laying out for her prodigal man a path

the color of blood,
and I snap the blue rubberband
hard against my well-thumbed translation,
think of how precious rubber was when
I was a boy back in Kansas folding the
Wichita Beacon, tossing its headlines

of landing after landing
on the pine receptive porches
of my customers. Iwo Jima. Guadalcanal.
Saipan. And it's bur oak mostly I admire,
it's that branch just over there I'd choose
if I had a choice to crouch on. And

Johnny Moulton with one limb missing
came marching home. So what I know is
mostly what I hope for, that my wife, that

other player in this sometime mythic game,
will greet me at the door,
in her hand a thick romance I trust

ends happily ever after, my fate meanwhile
no more than a scarf of sidewalk
bending home, sidewalk
patterned brightly with the letting go
of leaves so neutral in their
faithfulness, so red.

Two Trumpets in Sunlight

On a bright late-September morning
two trumpets in sunlight
blare softly—prelude to a college Forum.

Outside, between a wall of viburnum
and another of brick and mortar,
they seem almost to be sounding

without benefit of anything human—
no lip, no breath,
no tongue—

while inside a gathering throng
awaits an overview of slides:
The Roots of Western Civilization.

I stay to hear the silver duo perform
far beyond the moment
when the music's done,

I standing then in that same sunlight alone
those trumpets with their silver low
and high notes stood in,

and if I could I'd be moving
naked and barefoot
away from all hints of mummification,

beside me a goddess river flowing,
its bank a scroll of papyrus
without end,

blue sky free of gall and of worm-
wood, history ahead
as if it had yet to happen,

all things in a grandiose scheme
about to rise from their vast necropolis
into other lives, other dreams,

other trumpets in other sunlights mean-
while opening the lids of other sarcophagi
into the radicles of other times.

On a Porch Swing Swinging

On a porch swing swinging
I watch a warm
Indian-summer moon

give way to the long and
sudden shadows of evening.
From atop this well-tended

slope I follow a colt
on its way to horse
cavorting on an inland sea

of pasture. I imagine its
young haunches
bunching,

its young nostrils
flaring.
Between the yearling

and the swing where I am swinging
lies a crossroad,
and I think of the suicide

who might be buried there,
its grave like most of us
at last unmarked. Well,

life goes on and on, doesn't it,
the red on the bloom
of the flower

as if the blood that in
spite of frost
next year cannot be

stanched. The sun meanwhile
yields to the moment,
that temporary power.

On a porch swing swinging
I watch what darkness has
to offer. Inhaling deeply,

I close my eyes. Look:
no matter how fully
all of you disappear,

I see you.

Thinking More, Talking Less

It happens when the eyes,
paying strict attention, send a
swift connection to the brain:

that cottonwood just over there
must surely be a cousin
to the one I fell from,

cracking my left wrist, or
was it the right. No matter.
What does is that I missed the game

against Kiowa, my golden chance
to impress Elaine on the sideline
until death do us part. Small

wonder then that she fell for
Galen the quarterback,
that otherwise ineffectual slob

who scored twice himself and
passed for another. Life is like
that: fourth down and short yardage,

then the buddy you hate most
doesn't fumble. It's fun, actually,
this excursion of the static mind

into the dynamic past. When at last
you speak it's the bonebright
logic of the moment that heals,

that truly matters; looks like rain
coming in from the south,
how long has it been anyway

since you called your mother?

Oceanside, Early August

Because desire is what
we cannot choose but come to
we take the first step,
moving slowly from the busy room
onto the pier. For a long time
we watch the moon
make silverfish against the water,
the tide meanwhile doing
what it cannot otherwise do,
wash a dark beach darker.

Because desire is the cup
we cannot choose but drink
we concern ourselves
intensely with the body,
with what in our moments of most concern
the body might become.
On the beach at mid-day
a man with a metal detector
tells me how he hopes to find
an ancient doubloon, or, better yet, a ring,
something priceless from the shark-bait finger
of a lovely dark-haired stowaway,
something shiny and immortal
washed in from the salty green secret
we call ocean.

In a souvenir shop,
after another carafe of Chablis,
I buy what I tell myself I cannot
live without. Holding the conch shell

to my ear, its curled underside
pink as a woman's sex,
I hear the small incessant roar
of some distant body of water,
body that can't for its own
life's sake, and the sake
of all those unborn
liquid bodies so far beyond,
lie still.

Mowing the Sidewalk

Now my friend the philosopher,
who writes and sings his own sweet & sour
country tunes, tells me he has bought himself
a brand new reeltype pushmower, tells me
it's pretty much like the one he owned
in Oklahoma when his daddy preached there,
says that in those days his chief religious duty
was to keep the church lawn

clipped and raked—immaculate—and I can
more than hear him, can hear likewise
the snicksnicksnick of my own pushmower
leveling buffalo grass
beside the tiny stuccoed shed
where she kept also a file for me to brighten

the mower's blades with. My friend the philosopher
says that to live in the moment is to live
in eternity. He says, *Abstain from melody, you're
dead.* So I find myself pushing this brand new mower
over a stretch of sidewalk, its brand new blades
sounding snicksnicksnick, now allegro, now andante,
beside me my friend intoning a hybrid song—
I come to the back yard alone

while the dew is still on the bunchgrass. It's
simple, really: music is what happens
when two consenting edges make impeccable sounds
together. I meanwhile mow the sidewalk until
suddenly it's embarrassing. I stop, reverse the handle
to roll the mower with its reel inert

back to my friend the philosopher's
white wood-frame house. It is May. The morning,

bright, cloudless, smells thickly
of honeysuckle, of a neighborhood's overgrowth
of sweet viburnum. *Those who sail without oars,*
my friend the philosopher says,
keep on good terms with the wind, the mower
apparently knowing that much already,
its wheels on their new ballbearings purring
as if a far-off feline chorus

alleluia! at my slightest touch.

Walking to Work

At the corner of 56th and Huntington
a stranger in a pink blouse jogging
calls out, I like your poems! And she is gone
before we can discuss the matter further—

enjambment, extended metaphor, persona,
the occasional trisyllabic foot in otherwise
iambic measure. Gone too before
we can discuss those other primordial matters

that make the poetry possible—your dugout,
my dugout, the most appropriate nectar
to complement the fatted calf. I glance
over my shoulder to see a fleck of pink

bobbing smaller and smaller
against a horizon of bur oak and sycamore.
It's hickory, though, that this morning
I'm carrying to work, a stout well-seasoned

limb I ran across at the edge of Unionville
in north Missouri. All weekend
I shaped and sanded the stick,
smoothing its knob to velvet,

to what without suggesting it
my wife will no doubt think suggestive.
Three coats of tung oil then to darken it
to underscore the grain. I close my eyes

to learn how far this little piece of art
might take me. One iamb, two
iambs, three iambs, four. It's funny,
but in darkness the shape

of this maddening world makes sense—one foot
in front of the other, one crooked line
in time to be reckoned straight
from here to there.

Selling the World Book Door to Door

Not chiefly for the sake of three small girls
who greet me on the front porch,
certainly not for the sake of their long-gone father,
but for the sake of a mother with another mother's eyes—
she's the one who wants to learn
what's what,
yet seems to want to learn it somehow
indirectly: show me with word and picture
the history of bird, and I'll know more
of my own bird's untimely flight,
my own bright daughters'
fearful nesting.

She brings me coffee thick enough
to discourage slumber if not death itself
indefinitely. What she doesn't know is that
I am brand new on this job,
she my first customer. I am that slick,
she that desperate.

Each entry in the World Book, I tell her,
is written in language
suited to the subject, so that the reader,
all the way from bassinet to shroud,
can understand.

She understands.
She is beyond Mother Goose, she says,
though not quite ready for what's that French
guy? Baudelaire?

She is, she says,
drifting somewhere in between. So
show me with word and picture, she says,
the history of bird, and I'll know more...

Much later, my commission spent
on something important
I can't remember,
I imagine the mother with another mother's eyes
reading the World Book—not to her children,
not to her long-fled husband,
but to herself,
language suited to the subject,

the cock with its brilliant plumage,
the complicated history of retreat,
the way of all flesh reaching
for just one more beginning:
once upon a time.

Upon Learning of the Death
of My Hairdresser's Baby

—for Carmen

First I remember
how with her delicate hands
she waved me into the chair,
how as she snipped and trimmed and talked
she couldn't stop smiling.
She had lowered me
for the soap and the rinse,
and with my eyes closed
I had felt against my thigh
the heave and the swell of the child.
Rising, I spoke to her then in the mirror,
her young face roseate,
her dark eyes
quick like the fish we sprinkle food to
in a bowl of purest water.

And I remember next
how in the mirror
she paused from time to time
to press her hands against the weight inside her,
following with a comb the movement,
how she watched herself in the mirror, too,
how her dark eyes
flashed to see mine in the mirror watching her,
how the small bright aromatic room
enclosed us, each heartbeat
saying whatever it is the heart responds to.

And what I cannot remember I imagine,
the child imbalanced
fisting its disadvantage
onto the face of something huge and faceless,
sucking air that finally
isn't there.

Now my own house lies cool
in the aftermath of an early-morning rain.
In the mirror I am readying myself
for another day. Already April. Already
this sad white hair in need of another trim.
Yet how can I possibly take myself
to where she stands
to face her? Beyond the glass
I see my grandchildren
rising to romp their fortunate parts
into the beckoning teeth
of another morning. Excuse
not only me, I'll want to say, but
all of us (her delicate hands
waving me into the chair) for living.

After the Drunk Crushed My Father

what was left
wasn't much,
certainly not the automobile,

its brown body
inert
in a state of hunkered and

twisted shock, or
later the house, that shoebox,
or its bread and water

furnishings. But
something has to be
taken from death

to keep death
from taking everything,
so I select the rocker

my father upon his father's death
selected, one
half cherrywood, the other half

blood and knuckles and baling
wire, the man
who restores it speaking

with a thick Bavarian accent. Without
so much as the trace
of a boast

he says he knows by Jesus his
onions—which he does,
the rocker emerging too pure

to be altogether feasible. So
I'll have to work at it,
work at believing that

not only does it now exist
pristine and solid,
but that its existence

matters. Who, after all,
cares? Yet I think
I remember grandfather sitting

in this rocker, thick arms
working an accordion
whose bellows leaked considerable

air. Singing, I think it was,
shall we gather
at the river? He too was German

with a Dutchman's accent. And
his son, my father:
dead the officer surmised

before the Dodge came to rest
on its top, how
it lay there

heavy with its heavy internals
exposed, lay there
on the curve of its top

like the cradle in that
dead poet's poem
so endlessly rocking.

Treehouse

Through the kitchen window
I watch two boys
high in a black walnut

complete a treehouse
left to them by other renters
who last week loaded their blue

Apache and were
gone. They had
come to the neighborhood

as newlyweds,
had constructed the platform,
they said, as a high-rise extension

of their honeymoon. And
on more than several nights
I heard their voices

carrying clearly down,
syllables laced with laughter,
with the clinking of glasses. So

much for April into late September.
Now an Indian summer,
like the boys themselves,

has begun to happen,
and through both the window
and a falling of early-evening leaves

I can see their silhouettes at work,
hammers at the ends of anxious arms
tapping a muffled code

I think I'm at the edge of breaking.
Into a goblet I pour myself
the rough equivalent

of a Shirley Temple. O my life
now has an order and a plan:
to stand here sipping and watching

until the full moon rises, until
with its light it opens the door
the boys will have closed and with a cob

secured. But I am neither here nor there,
neither building nor leaving
town. And though already

I am dead on my feet
I have the dead's advantage.
I have all night.

Singing Hymns with Unitarians

The Unitarian sings with a mouth
almost closed,
words from Jefferson and Thoreau

streaming in a duality of breath
neither hot nor cold
from the Unitarian's transcendental

nostrils. And it is not possible
to be among the congregation
without loving both the creator

and the creation. In the beginning
didn't all of us begin? And
doesn't that include the hummingbird

feeding at that fleck of purple
flowerhead in the stained-
glass window?

I open my mouth to chew at words
already chewed
by a raft of ancestors.

The hummingbird too grows fat
on its own deception. When all of this
is finished, will anything matter?

The word on the papyrus page?
The note at the wing of the bird
as it lifts away?

A City Waking Up

An early-morning shower
softens the sounds
of a city waking up,

south wind moving the leaves,
moving the raindrops
into the leaves,

and for a long morning
I lie in bed
a wide white sheet

thinking of rain, thinking
of others and what others
thought of rain,

grandmother washing her hair
in rainwater
caught in a galvanized tub,

Father with a funnel
pouring rainwater
into the cells of the battery

in the Model-T, itinerant preacher
back home on impulse, or perhaps
goaded by some holy tine,

leading his flock outside
and into the eye of a gullywasher,
there to perform a wholesale act

of baptism, all eyes skyward but
closed, sprinkling and immersion
taking each worshipper down

to essential bone. And that legend
of W.C. Fields on his
last boozy legs,

reading the Bible, *looking,* as he
said, *for loopholes,*
praying he'll die to the sound

of rain on the rooftop. And
how the prayer was answered,
thanks to friends

who joined the garden hose
to compassion. And
of Wendell Berry

on his homestead in Kentucky,
writing of rain, writing
especially of rain after drought,

calling his waking late at night
to the pattering of rain
My sweetness. And

it's my sweetness, too, this
early-morning shower
in early September,

a city waking up, school children
dumped from the bus
like so many hilarious crustaceans,

my body adrift on a river of bed
going south to the sea
going nowhere.

Benediction

Somewhere deep in the grove of cottonwoods
an owl with its dark split tongue
pronounces an end to day,
and the river,
that great brown hussy, that gadabout,
moves on,
its motion its wisdom,
its wayward parts at last becoming one,
its crooked path as seen from the proper height
the soft deflections of a tireless line.

If you love me,
stand with me
here behind the locust
to watch the rising of a full marriage moon.
See? There it is, just over there,
ascending that leaf, just over there,
ascending that limb,
in silhouette ascending the very tip of that perfect thorn.

Can the sound that the bird makes be our own,
the water in the river
that home that can't stay home?

If you love me,
lie with me
between the owl and the river,
beneath the awful wheeling of a marriage moon.
Let the sound that the bird makes be our own.
Let the water in the river
be our home that can't stay home.

Let there be no move, not now, not ever,
to put an end to end.
Let the earth, proud woman, old friend, roll over.

Let the dance begin.

This Tree, This Hackberry

This tree, this hackberry
marks the center of the homestead well
the youngest of the Holcomb offspring
dallied into. The rescue effort failed.
Without a curbing, the walls,
as if on cue, had buckled in.
Just too much stress, they said,
against that vertical of mud and sand.

Fred the father planted the tree,
Joseph the middle son
the first of many to cut it down.
Behind a brace of mares
its branches made a vast ungainly harrow
to skim away the bunchgrass
on a long narrow strip of new-cut ground.

Imagine the final step into darkness
deep as a mother's dream.
Imagine the roots of the hackberry,
loco for something damp and sweet,
reaching ten full fathoms downward,
there to discover a huddle of bone and marrow
that in another life had answered
to Rebecca Lynne.

Or would have answered,
had she not been so all-fired busy with the butterfly,
remarking the brilliance of the orange on its wing
under a high and mighty Cherry County, in Nebraska, sky.

Not Such a Bad Place to Be

True, the wind in the elms
is sometimes enough almost
to tip the scales
in the wrong direction,
and when the water gathers itself
into an onslaught down the big branch,
even Christkiller Burhman
goes to his knees in the pool hall,
pleading for fins.
And the soil:
true, it often takes back
more than a portion
of that which it gives,
it being in cahoots, one suspects,
with the water and the wind.
Which leaves us with
the daily vexation of fire:
how it can warm to madness
that very same skull
it enlightens.

Even so,
it's not such a bad place to be.
At certain moments
an element swells the lungs with something akin to faith:
and all else falls away
as if dark appendages let loose
when the child stops dreaming.
And we know what we know so clearly
that not even the heft
of whatever follows
can altogether obscure
the meaning.

Killing the Swallows

Dusk.
I sit with my brother
on a chair of baled straw
at the center of the haymow,
counting rocks.
We will divide the total
as carefully as if candling eggs,
then decide from whom, and from how many,
to draw the blood.

The rocks have come from the pasture,
from small knobs of ungrassed earth
washed clean by rain.
The swallows do not know this:
that with each rain
a fresh span of death
surfaces, then in the sunlight
fairly gleams.

Nor do they know that darkness
means more, perhaps, than a brief sleep.
Thus they dip their narrow wings,
as if layers of innocence,
into the haymow and
onto the topmost beam.

We sense more than see them,
my brother like a small towheaded priest
over his pyramid of stones,
I thumbing the switch
on the flashlight, waiting.
The birds, ignorant of rain and darkness,

know little more of light:
they disappear soft as down
into the struts and the rafters.
We will kill as many of them
as we have stomachs for,
and call it, if anything, man's need.
We will trust then to the cats
to do what remains
of the honors.

Thus we wait.
And the ritual occurs,
no more untoward than breathing.
The rock from the slingshot
follows its bright light upward,
finds its mark in the seed-heavy
belly of the bird.
Again and again the ritual occurs:
occurs the ritual, again and again and again,
sun rising, sun delivering,
sun going down.

In the gathering shadows
tribesmen touch their fingers
to spears honed bright
with spittle and flint.
They will depend upon
an ageless cluster of daughters,
the Pleiades, to cap their day.
They believe that man, more fortunate,
had been born in wraps of fur or feathers,
and they are far too lean,
and far too proud in blood,
ever to turn away.

For My Wife's Father

More and more my wife's father
sleeps in his chair,
as if practicing.
But I am not deceived.
I have seen him
at the muting of a single word
revive,
his osseous hands toss off
their fitful tics.
I have watched his eyes
return from the water's edge,
become sharp as spoons.
Those who catch him in his chair,
at sleep, should not be deceived.
He is not practicing.
He is at the water's edge,
listening to the sucking of the carp
and with them gathering.

Thanksgiving

Aunt Vivian leads the charge
against the paper plate:
eat noodles off something like that
and you deserve
whatever brand of scurvy it is
you pass away from.

Steam above the platter of roasted turkey
portends an eruption:
Vesuvius in fullest flower,
all over again.

Uncle Howard's new blue shirt
gapes like a goldfish
shortly above his beltbuckle.
Pass the potatoes, sweet William,
and while you're at it
throw in some gravy
and a fistful of hot rolls.

The flesh on Beulah's upper arm
hangs so low it
brushes the broccoli.
Iced tea gurgles like a busy drain
in the small arid throat
of Cousin Eileen.

Eldon remembers when ham and beans and Monday
were the same.
Slim Jimmy, attempting once more
to chink the gaps

under the slack of his nettled skin,
devises a totem of apple pie,
sliced cheese, chocolate cake,
vanilla and butter brickle
ice cream.

Easy there on the rum, Grandma:
Marvin the Would-Be Missionary
likes his strawberries
tart as a sermon.

You can do the dishes, Vivian.
I'm going outside
to dropkick a football
through the Virgin Martha's window.
Curious I am, and lonesome,
to know the sound of something trapped
escaping.

Drifting

> They that go down to the sea in ships, that do busi-
> ness in great waters; these see the works of the Lord,
> and his wonders in the deep.
>
> —*Psalms 107, 23-24*

Going down to no great sea
To do no great business,
I lie relaxed on this
Moving water that knows
Its way even on windless

Days between pastured banks
And around fills of wispy
Shifting sand. The one-man
Rubber raft beneath me knows
No weight. It is seamed like peel

To the juice of my unmighty
River, and I to it. Face up,
Eyes closed, legs trailing
Like jointed driftwood,
I give myself to the river.

      The world is surplus,
      And only surplus matters.

The current tells me with
Its brief maelstroms that we
Are moving, while not even
A full sun can deny
Me darkness. I turn slowly,

Whorling from the sun, feeling
Change as the river changes,
We vulcanized to softness
Under undulations
Lighter than the lightness

Of cottonwood seed on water.
Peace is this, and the quick liquid note
Of a contiguous meadowlark,
The small sound hovering like flotsam
On the sun-washed crown of the river.

Oceans fail;
All ships of war have settled.

For less than sixteen dollars
I own what matters. Inflated
With my own breath, with air
That has touched all shores, my raft
Like forgiveness bears me up. We are

Breadless on no troubled waters,
Being blessed by the Navy's compassion
For leftovers that need
Somewhere to go, and someone
To go with, while waiting.

So in smallness we vagrants wait on,
In dizzying silence
Thankful for silence and smallness,
For the patient, diurnal sun,
For the current that flows in the river.

The USN is infinite
In its concern for remnants.

It is not my no great sea
That I am on, doing
No great business for no one
Great—except perhaps
A bit for the meadowlark,

Who perhaps accepts my sight
As I his sound. How could
He see me except that I
Be here? With long bare legs
I wash the water clean,

And with my outstretched hands
I give the river bones
To part its current with.
My hair stirs stillness
Into a slow cool breeze.

We live by drifting
Only on borrowed things.

Beside brush the current darkens.
Half asleep, I feel the shadows.
The wispy sand is high.
I shake myself into daylight,
And the bright world focuses.

My legs have turned the water
Shallow. The raft scrapes sand.
In drunkenness I stand

To find the lost current,
To portage over time

And over glistening grit
The confidence that though
Going down to no great sea
To do no great business
Is the business of no great king,

> The world is surplus,
> And only surplus matters.
> Oceans fail;
> All ships of war have settled.
> The USN is infinite
> In its concern for remnants.
> We live by drifting
> Only on borrowed things.

Epitaph for a Grandfather

Fifty paces short of the designated grave
the hearse takes a wrong turn,
and the driver, drenched and apologetic,
signals the pallbearers out of their cars:
and my grandfather is bumped
more carefully than possible
to that place where rock and gumbo
have been, for the moment,
worried aside.

In this land of small lots and persimmon
there is no such thing as looking back:
the preacher, from Ecclesiastes,
settles my grandfather into its wry, inclusive scheme,
and before the last fine grain of Scripture
scours the coffin,
several of the stoutest mourners' eyes
already are at the axles of their Fords and Chevys,
wanting out.

Nebraska: This Place, These People

All across the sandhills
and down the panhandle
and back across again
and up the Missouri into Omaha,
this place, these people
bloom like firebushes.

An old woman in Wahoo punches her thumb
into the soil,
and fourteen babies in
Weeping Water
give thanks.

Atop the capitol at Lincoln
a statue with a satchel at his side
is always about to scatter
the promise of next year's breakfast.

A young lover not far from Thedford
spitshines the manure
on his best boots.

Valentine opens itself to sunshine
hot as a kiss.

Catfish and carp are warming themselves
like beach bums
in the shallows of the
Platte and the Elkhorn and the Loup.
From the south-southwest a breeze
trembles cottonwood seed

like friendly flak
toward a Dakota border.

A covey of quail
struts the main street of Brownville
like vaudeville troupers up from the dead,
claiming first privilege.

On the outskirts of Macy Reservation,
in the weeds by the highway,
an ancient Indian and a shag buffalo
whisper to each other
through the thin skin
of an outnumbered nickel.

Nebraska.
This place, these people
blaze like firebushes.

Water and soil and wind,
color and light and heat:

something forever plump and firm
above the ground,
the itch forever
of something small but ripening

underneath.

Christmas 1939

The car sits
burdened in the
driveway: when
the last bundled
body settles onto
the back seat the
back axle snaps.

Such is Christ-
mas, such the
beginning of each
mysterious trip to
grandfather's dis-
tant farm. Father
circles the low-
slung vehicle,
kicking each tire.
What he is saying
darkens the air,
accelerates a
gathering of clouds.

We have a cousin
who drives fast
and who knows the
Ford dealer in
Argonia. And the
miracle is not
that someone came
along to give us
life beyond the
life we never asked
for, but that

cousin in little
under an hour
returns. A miracle
too that nut and
bolt and black
grease at the elbow
come at last together.

Three miles north
of the Barber County
line the snow
thickens. Christ,
if it isn't one damn
thing it's a dozen.
Father's breath
brings the clouds
all the way inside
and onto the wind-
shield.

The humming of the
heater begins to
turn me to slush.
The miracle is that
there is no end
to miracles. My
little brother in
his sleep grins
like a perfect
moron. I am not
far behind. What
we yield to is the
insolence of faith:
when we waken we
will be there.

Sunday Morning

This morning I am trotting the route,
my father not far away in the old Ford coupe,
its heater humming all the hymns
I ever knew the tunes to,
Sunday papers on the seat at his right
like a massive passenger,
and the pace from beginning to end
doesn't vary, I at a slow heavy trot,
the old Ford in low gear
growling in the clear bright icy
January air like a good large watchdog
creeping on the rollers of its haunches,
always about to lurch, yet never lurching,
my breath meanwhile in measured bursts
preceding me, fogging the eyes,
chilling the face, all things
in the early aftermath of sunrise
a most delicate syncopation, the smoke
from my father's cigarette (I'm
trotting now beside the car,
reaching for papers to fill again
that hollow in my arm) sweet
as the tune being hummed by the heater,
sweet and as warm as the tune
being hummed by the heater,
I trotting beside the open window
catching both the warmth and the song,
and my father, silent behind the wheel,
helping me this morning with the route,
giving me a hand to relieve
this impossible Sunday morning

weight, laying that hand on my shoulder
to wake me, to tell me that the bitter
cold is here, to say, without
my asking, I'll take you.

Walking the Tracks

It's the shortest
route to the sand-
pit, the perfect
chance to fill my
pockets with rocks
for the bullfrogs.
I have one hook,
one bobber, one
length of grocery
twine, one sinker,
one dozen night-
crawlers secure in
a Prince Albert can.

And the sun strik-
ing the iron, strik-
ing and striking:
half blinded I miss
my cutoff, keep
right on toward
Kiowa County
walking.

The long ride home
on the slow freight
isn't long enough.
I dangle lost legs
as if sashweights
over the edge of
the flatcar. Smell
of cut alfalfa,

slant of bird-
wing, dusk.

The freight with
its flat wheels
limps into town. O
mother I have been
everywhere. Listen,
listen to me now. I
know everything.

Kicking Leaves

All day I have been walking
and kicking leaves,
not paying any attention
to time or direction,
so that when the sun
becomes an orange wafer
at the edge of my left shoulder,
and I cross over the line
into that other land,
I have to smile,
the leaves there as if
the leaves from home,
embarrassed, brisk, compatible.
And I turn to watch you
kicking the same leaves
I kicked, you behind me
kicking and catching up,
catching up, kicking
so many of those lovely leaves
I can't get enough of
you behind me.

Mowing the Lawn for the Last Time

I do it shortly after sunrise,
after the first hard freeze,
each swath a shredding
of leaf and of blade and of frost,
each swath so green, so perfect
I pause time and again to look
down the row to inhale as well as
to see it, to take it all in.

And the sound of the mower: a red
Piper Cub against a blue sky,
circling. Which is why
I do not hear my wife
at first when she calls me.

We sit on elm stumps drinking black coffee
from thick white porcelain cups
left from the days of her dead father's
café. I remember the waitress
whose face, it was said, could sour
milk, how the regular customers
loved her. We hold the cups
with both hands, leaning our faces
into them. The morning
for a few moments with us
stands still. We are very happy.

Uncertain the Final Run to Winter

Summer,
a fat horse
tender against the spurs.

Now as the last edge of autumn
hangs precipiced in yellow on the trees
the animal sees the sudden space and shies.
I sense the ropy girth go loose:
uncertain the final run to winter.

Between the halt and the beginning
lies the gap,
familiar to the eye
as palm to pommel.

My lean horse balks: ahead,
the wide white skylessness of space.

Not knowing where mount and rider end,
or where they come together,
I see myself as statue weathered,
sitting its saddle like an Ichabod.

Cleaning Out My Dead Grandfather's Barn

A sudden flash of light
No larger than a dime
Told me that human hands
Had worn the pommel to newness
Where old leather had been.

But today the human hands
Went dead a final time.
Piling harness and saddle away,
Cantle and stirrup, singletree,
Checkrein, blinder and hame,

I saw the sudden flash
Of Granddad in the coin
Of light: his hands without
Splotches lay like the power
Of horseflesh tugging to join

Gray seasons to this fresh September.
Then heartlessly the hands
Went dull: no more. Just the
Heavy hide of cracked
Harness, a broken bellyband,

And cruppers rubbed with the brown
Of fifty years of dung.
I piled it all in the pickup
And drove it quickly away
From the low-angled autumn sun.

December 8, 1941

Sound travels to tell us
Not of something ended
But of something begun.
So in the early morning,

During the hour for arithmetic,
Jackie Dellman stands alone,
Privileged in the cloakroom,
Crying without raising his hands

Before a clear bright pane
Of window. Yesterday the Japanese
Bombed his big brother at
Pearl Harbor; today the sound of the

Rising Sun is rich with bravado
And fear and the slight vibrant
Embarrassment of seated schoolboys
Calculating their new classmate,

Who only two days ago celebrated Friday
By bloodying the taller nose
Of a red-haired confident
Fifth grader, but who now,

On this peculiar Monday morning,
Weeps at the window with the
Cloakroom door open, weeps
With his victorious fists

Dangling like bandages at his sides,
His bare grief confounding all
Human equations. Yet I with others
Hear and work with it; it

Enters my wooden desk
To travel up my spine
To finally force a whiteness
Upon the foreign fingers that

Clutch at pencils. There seems
To be no stopping it,
It that rose how long
Before the rising of the

Rising Sun, that slid inviolable
Over calm international airways
At how many hundred feet-per-second
To tell the Emperor that he owns

The world and must dispose of
Jackie Dellman's brother,
To become the whistle of bomb-fins
On a soundless Sunday morning,

To be the keen of boyhood
And the wail of silent
Bewildered mathematicians,
Their long division growing forever

Longer: who in this conflagration
First spoke of fire? And who
Will be the last to shout its heat
Into the cool quotient of emptiness?

Carry A. Nation came into our house and filled it
With her meagerness. She was hung full-fleshed
Against the flowered wallpaper of our living-room,
And Mrs. Wilma Hunt, who brought her, gave each
Of us a little wooden hatchet. "John Barleycorn
Is the Devil," Mrs. Wilma Hunt said. And
By dropping worms head-
First into alcohol she taught us
To hate him. "Now let me tell
You," she said, "about the LTL..."

She taught us the Loyal
Temperance Legion song, all of it, then killed
Another worm and served refreshments. Our house
Had never been so full. There were all of us, with
Carry on the wall-
Paper: Kool-Aid, Cookies, Song,
Something-New-to-Hate—
And several dead worms
Curled in alcohol.

Town Team

The local jocks back home in Attica
seem more than amply snugged.

At first base a stomach extends itself
to scoop a low throw, like a gunslug,
from the dust.

The shortstop moves like a sweet fat fairy
to his right or left,
his sneakers leaking ballbearings.

Outfielders jog for several days to their positions,
pivot like bloated ballerinas,
doff their caps,
then jog for several days back to the dugout.

The infield is a squat and pussel-gutted chain.
Round faced and red, it
chews its tongue and
spits practically perfect daisies.

The pitcher trembles the mound with a headshake:
he wants another sign.
The catcher, wide as a sandcrab,
sweats marbles.

At the plate
a batter settles into his stance
like a tender, untapped keg.

Toots Slocum

Black magic yet in the words Toots Slocum,
who like all natural incomparables
came into this world
with the same basic apparatus
she circumcised our backfield with.
How else explain the opening loss to Kiowa?
And the way we ran at Medicine Lodge!
Goons, goons, goons,
gooneyes aglint like little silver marbles,
goonhands bearing the pigskin
like a brown leather chalice
directly to the sideline,
to the airborne X where Toots Slocum
sprawled upright,
arrested in midcheer,
her breasts defiant inside a lettersweater,
a triangle of her tights
exposed and magnetized,
more luminous, more precious than a goalpost.

Thus while the center and the guards,
the tackles and the ends plowed straight ahead,
the backfield scurried like lemmings to the shoreline,
to the open and upthrown form
of Tootsie Slocum.

For Toots never did screw
an interior lineman,
a discipline that added charm to charm:
though it also probably had a lot do
with Galen Tucker's suicide,
not to mention Fairport's tragic
0-8 season.

Saunders County Barn

Try to ignore that Saunders County barn,
the one with the slatted, broken back,
where swallows in the dusk are homing.

Don't ask who the grandfather was
that called his milkcows to those brittle boards,
whether he had one offspring, or a dozen.

Don't concern yourself with the color of his teeth,
or inquire into the type of wood he fired
to burn the mortgage. Nor his wife:

whether she kept her wits past sixty,
or as a new bride drew blood when she
looked upon the back forty and bit her lip.

Nor their child, or children:
whether after one more final coat of paint
he/she/they hired an auctioneer. Or didn't,

and so hung on to be buried north of the toolshed.
Don't care whether the barn smells yet of dung,
whether the stanchions are yet slick

from the rubbings of cows' necks.
Don't bother even to ask after the swallows,
whether their droppings are mellowing in brittle hay.

Tell yourself that it has been a long and dusty day,
that you must reach Wahoo by nightfall.
Thus, with firmness, tell the barn to go away.

Then glance at your rear-view mirror,
where, like a midget posing, relieving itself into the wind,
the barn grows smaller and smaller, then disappears.

Concentrate now on the road ahead.
Do not waste yourself on anything
lost, neglected, absent, weathered, or dead.

Collecting for the Wichita Beacon

The first house I step into
has this picture of a Marine corporal
atop the radio,
dungaree jacket pressed to a fare-you-well,
cap tilted back cockeyed
confident.

Tossing aside the paper,
the young woman, eyes so very dark, so
large, so downright beautiful,
says we are winning,
says that in spite of Wake Island and Guadalcanal
it is only a matter of time.
She tells me this again as, fumbling in her purse,
she comes up with three quarters and a forerunner
to the Franklin D. Roosevelt memorial dime.

Before releasing the coins into my hand
she moves the tip of an index finger
ever so lightly
against my palm. O
she has seldom been quite this frightened, never
this lonely. She thinks maybe, honestly,
this time she is going all the way
crazy. Against my face
her kiss is how much more
than a mother's.

I am not there to do any type of singing
when the telegram comes.
Sixty-seven customers, sixty-seven screen-

doors under relentless siege
hanging on.
And time to collect again.
And John Wayne shot again by a slant-eyed sniper.

And my face, where the kiss was, napalm burning.
And I cannot so much as give you the time of day,
and I cannot tell you, not even
to the nearest war,
how old I am.

Sowing the Whirlwind

Grandmother Moulton heavy against a crutch
receives her copy of the paper
as if a blessing, her lips
thanking God incessantly
for most everything—for
her grandson John's diving, not jumping,
into that crater at Omaha Beach,
burst of bullets shattering
only the right ankle,
for the end of the war by whatever means,
and I am not halfway around the route
before Hiroshima becomes a word
I was born with never to understand.

Each customer is a study in ice,
though early August in my town in Kansas
swelters the white cotton shirt
that swelters the skin.
Each customer stands on bare feet
on the unpainted pine
of that porch most accessible,
one arm extended, across the mouth
the wary suggestion of a grin.
I am for this one early evening
important beyond even the flaming lipstick
of Ruby Shoemaker's dissension. O receive
from the hand of the older son
of Ralph and of Katie Marie
both the lines and what lies between:
that something larger than mere imagination
has taken place, that the heat this day,

this hour, this moment, though insufferable,
is but a beginning.
Each customer thaws enough to work the fingers
to accept what moves in the shimmering heat
like a minnow
mushroomed at the edge
of a lessening pond.

Elwood Anderson, who is queer in the head,
hammers ten-penny nails into an old crosstie
whenever he has more
than his thick queer tongue can say.
Just how windless is this windless day?
By the time I give old man Fenton the news
already I can hear the ping
carrying clearly over cowlot, over lawn, over alley.
One ping to one nail, one ping
driving one nail so precisely, so deeply home.
How many nails can one tie comprehend?
Elwood Anderson, so sure of himself
he uses a ballpeen,
has eyes the sheen of nailheads
returning the sun,
but as far as I know
he has never seen his way to subscribing
to the *Wichita Beacon*.

Bless O Lord these gifts
which we are about to receive
through thy merciful bounty. Amen.
This is one of so many cadences
I pump my purple Monarch bike to.
O Jesus is the rock

in a weary land, a weary land, a weary land,
O Jesus is the rock
in a weary land,
a shelter in the time of storm.
That's another.

Inside the Champlin Station
I folded sixty-seven papers to a different,
far more convoluted rhythm.
Scanned each headline sixty-seven times
to hear it
scan. Atomic bomb
dropped on Japan; President warns
of a rain of ruin.
At each downward thrust of my right foot
something in the ankle pops,
and with Johnny Moulton I dive, not jump,
into the crater. Shattered the anklebone,
spared to fight another day
the brain. Scientific landmark of the century
realized. And I remember that movie
about the Sullivans,
all of them going down with their ship,
brother upon brother, the language
of starboard and port and the steady
deep-green gurgle
of death. Why,
when my friend Bullard said Sharkbait,
didn't I slug him?

Though almost dusk
the day sits

hot as the sun, rising,
hot as the rising sun. We have spent
two billion dollars on the greatest
scientific gamble in history —
and won.

I do not stop for a game of one-on-one
with Bullard. I think instead of the cool breeze
blowing down from the ceiling fan
in the pool-hall, the clean click
of ball against ball. Our town is a dry town.
I was a snooker shark I swear at eleven.
Did I mention that Grandmother Moulton's lips
never stop moving? Johnny came limping home again,
died of cancer around nineteen sixty-seven.
When Mr. Truman announced the bomb aboard the Augusta,
one of the crewmen said
I guess I'll be home sooner now.
Ah, home, where are you?

In five days I'll be thirteen,
in thirty-seven years
fifty,
by which date I shall have learned
the following: the code name
for the experimental explosion
in New Mexico (July one six)
was Trinity.

Starboard. Port.
And the Sullivan boys
sharkbait going under,
so steady their deep-green death-green
gurgling.

I cannot speak for tomorrow.
An impenetrable cloud of dust today
hides practically everything. Have we in fact
sowed the whirlwind? O Mrs. Sullivan, O babies
still in the bellies of the Honshu women,
take solace in the smaller print.
Shaving Lotion Shortage
Expected to End
Soon.

Mabel Cleveland takes her paper
with something more than ice
at the edge of her grin.
Bless you, anyway, Mabel Cleveland,
and your husband, Shorty,
and your twin snooty daughters Anna and Alma
who even today are more or less
somewhere, more or less
fully grown. Speaking of which:
I love all of you more than I ever can.

Here's another.
There's a German in the grass
with a bullet up his ass.
Push it in, pull it out,
Uncle Sam, Uncle Sam.

Home is where Elwood Anderson sends each ten-penny nail,
ping the sound I go to sleep by,
wild in my little wreckage
to understand.

Waiting to Jell

We are waiting to jell.
Woods, with his easy, high-hanging hookshot,
is somewhere south of the Mason-Dixon line.
In the heart of southcentral Kansas
Bullard speaks gently to his bulldozer,
coaxing it deeper and deeper into the earth.
Anspaugh is bottle-feeding a naked caveman
with Paul's first letter to the Corinthians.
Skeeter, an instrument in one eye
like a telescoped lens,
is putting together a necklace
made of dimestores.
And Kloefkorn, having slopped the hogs,
turns up the wick on the lamp
and, with a fresh quill
plucked from the nether eye
of a noncommittal goose,
writes on and on about waiting to jell,
he himself waiting
while recalling Bo Spoon, the coach,
who filled every halftime
with the same incredible prediction:
One of these times, boys, we are going to jell.

We won three and lost seventeen.
But the diamonds in Bo Spoon's eyes
cut through and halved our doubts,
left us reaching for season upon season,
for times and places and turnabouts
then, as today, unborn.

Thus we move and breathe
and pivot our understandings,
Woods at center, Bullard and Anspaugh forwards,
Skeeter and Kloefkorn at the guards.
The Bulldogs, the starting five, waiting to jell.

Dust meanwhile swirls at the feet.
Coins, like rain, reverse a trend,
roll as if players to stage center,
wobble slowly down, evaporate.
Spoon, having snapped his fingers
and popped his left palm,
smacks the inside of one Oxford heel
against the inside of the other.
It is halftime.
We are far, far behind.
The thick, steamy smell of socks
leaks from consumed rubber shoes.
One of these times, boys, we are going to jell.
And when we do...

And the fine long fingers on Woods' right hand
release the ball:
it rises slowly to the peak of its arc,
and by the time it reaches southcentral Kansas
Bullard already is on his way home,
the snort in the nose of his bulldozer
quiet as grass.
Anspaugh, pointing to an orange omen in the sky,
shifts his text to Ecclesiastes,
and Skeeter, returning from one more meeting of the board,
thanks his lucky stars that what goes down
sometimes comes up.

And the ball by now
is so near the front lip of the basket
that the multitude hushes.
With a quill freshly dipped,
Kloefkorn writes the ball
over the lip and into the stale,
magic center of the hoop.
Slowly then it descends, seams turning slowly,
and slowly the net fluffs and rises and falls,
and the home portion of the gathering slowly
erupts, comes slowly to its feet,
arms slowly outstretched,
mouths bursting slowly with tongues,
all of them shouting slowly Blood! Blood! Blood!
But Bullard, bone-weary and smelling of Lysol,
is curled into sleep at midcourt.
Anspaugh walks off with a cheerleader
in the direction of Reno.
Skeeter, having removed his tennis shoes,
has marked them down to half price.
And Woods, as if witching for water,
extends his long hairless arms
to follow his fingers
out of the auditorium
and along the white broken stripes
on the south-bound pavement.

Alone, Kloefkorn signals the crowd
to remain calm.
With the aid of a bullhorn
he announces that he has sent out
for a new lampwick and a goose unmarked.
Already he can see the fresh ink

forming thin, sharp lines
at the base of the busy quill.
The face of Bo Spoon emerges, focuses,
enters the dressing room.
It is halftime.
We are far, far behind.
One of these times, boys, we are going to jell.
And when we do...

Breathing, I must believe.
Believing, I wait.

One of Those

—for Ralph, my father

1.
In his best monotone
my father sings the Great Speckled Bird,
humming those lines he doesn't remember,
or, more likely, never knew,
then for a change of pace
breaks into the Wabash Cannonball.

He is lost in whatever it is
he is doing: patching a screendoor,
affixing a plugin, rearranging the junk
in the cellar. He takes a break
to roll a cigarette from a can of Raleigh.
He licks the tissue firmly into place,
strikes a kitchen match
against a latch on his overalls,
with a deep inhalation
turns the coarse tobacco
into a delicate rod of ash.
I'm saving up coupons, he sings,
to buy one of those; a coupon redeemer,
I'll die, I suppose.

I suppose. Yet in my longer night
I work to believe what lies
beyond the fine print
on the depleting can:
Hang on! The best surprise of them all
is yet to come!

2.

I enter my father's house
to gather the coupons
to redeem them. I am, quite suddenly,
fifty. Yet I must believe that
had my father mailed the coupons
all awkward corners would have been
set straight: severed fingers,
floating kidney, double hernia,
the quarrel with my mother
that night in the bedroom,
its first word a wedge
that the weight of time, near
penniless and obtuse,
could not stop driving.

3.

Somewhere in some grandiose warehouse
must surely wait the gift to restoration.
With a flashlight I find bundle on bundle
of coupons, each tied with white thread
taken (O how dream links guess to memory!)
from the old black Singer's bobbin.

The beam of light is alive with dust.
It guides me, begins to control me. It is
my first large dog returned
whose leash I stranglehold
to be led by,
uncanny eye disclosing coupons and
coupons, until, quite suddenly,
through a butterfly snag in a windowblind,
the first sharp sign of morning. And its light

strikes the face of my father. He watches me
watching him. He is almost smiling.
What he will say when he speaks
is that dusty text so long sealed shut
at the base of the brain: son,
it has been such a long long time.

4.
Meanwhile, there is the silence, meanwhile
then the start of the monotone. Thin old man
with green eyes sharp as spoons
singing, almost smiling, bulge
at the crotch of his blue washpants
that truss that forever
has held him in. Tell me:
what can an old man possibly know
that a younger man however old
doesn't? Until, quite suddenly, the room
brightens to a halo. I blink
to see the coupons gone. Father,
I understand. Father,
with three short steps
I could touch your hand. Christ,
I cannot help myself. I am singing it
truly to know it with him.

Cornsilk

—for Alva Foil Baker

My wife's father is about to be buried.
The minister is saying something
rapidly becoming final.
Under the edge of the canopy,
canopy bluer far than any Kansas sky's blue,
I hold my grandson of almost sixteen months.
A steady southern breeze upblows his hair,
cornsilk of the very highest order

suspended, and I turn us slowly clockwise
because I am playing the game called
viewing the world through the upblown suspended
cornsilk hair of my grandson: O
cornsilk the Chinese elm and the wide green catalpa,
cornsilk the red earth fresh from plowing,
cornsilk the high August sun, the western horizon,
cornsilk the buffalo grass and the near nervous

cornsilk sweep of the kingbird,
and under the spray of red carnations
cornsilk the mind's last memory of my wife's father,
all the days of his life recounted
as if strands of cornsilk
moving light and eternal
in a warm fixed partial
hour of wind.

Waiting for the Bus at 63rd and Huntington

No wind this morning,
not so much as the slightest move
from a single leaf on the cottonwood.
The rainclouds, after a slow heavy night,
seem spent, seem satisfied now
describing the blue of scattered sky
beyond them.

And waiting for the bus at this corner
at 63rd and Huntington
I cannot inhale deeply enough
to both catch it and keep it: your body
so fresh, so revived from its shower,
ankle and thigh, belly, nipple, lip, lash,
and the brief gracious scent
from the white flower drenched
on the linden.

From Within the First House

From within the first house
I looked out one early morning
to see the milkcow
looking back at me,
her eyes huge and clear,
a tuft of green dung
clinging to her udder.
She stood wide and solid,
the veins in her neck
explosive—
yet something in the chewing
of her cud suggested mystery.
So out of myself
I found myself uncurling:
into the window's glass,
into the dawn of air and eye
beyond the glass repairing.
And here is what the cow
was wondering:
why her milker
had left her standing there
unstripped
that pale, peculiar evening:
had dragged the bucket of milk,
aslosh and bottom heavy,
across the lot
and over the yard
and up the steps
and out of everything
except for hearing.
And then the silence.

And then the night.
And then the early morning.

And then the screaming.
And then the hands forever
of someone else,
the forehead at the flank
less warm, less reassuring.
And I said to the cow:
I was born that morning.
I arrived trailing the seventh scream.
And the one who left you standing
is my mother.
She is asleep now,
and I am beside her,
at her breast, beholding.
And listen:
this is the first time in all my days
that I have seen things clearly.
And O how fresh, how sweet the world is!
It is a house of milk and tongue
and eye and skin
and breath and breast and quilt
and fingertips and dung,
and that is all it is.

And that is everything!

On a Hot Day After Rain

On a hot day after rain
our cowlot fairly simmers.
Franklin and I, in high-top rubber boots,
each with a length of sumac,

prod the Jersey this way and that,
up and down, back and forth,
mud and manure those staples
kneaded by split steps into gumbo.

The fence around the cowlot
is made of thick planks, creosoted—
father says no doubt to keep some former owner's
blue-blooded big-balled bull in.

We do not have one. Only the Jersey,
and a mulberry tree twenty feet I'd say
from the fence. The lot,
each square inch pocked and thus

with the mark of our own beast
branded, is where my brother and I
first learn the thrill of smell,
we jumping in tandem from the fencetop

to meet a grain-sack swing on its
backswing rising swiftly
toward us, our weight
at the instant of impact

bending as if to break that largest limb
on the mulberry. Eventually, of course,
one knot or the other gives way,
and with Franklin I roll in the swamp,

with Franklin, my brother, in the swamp,
both holding as if for dear sweet life
that other betrayed life between us.
Hello stench of burlap,

effluvium of grain.
Hello mud and manure, hello dollops of water that
purpled in season with berries
out-blind the sun.

Hello first hour of those first ten million years
of skull becoming man,
the brain in the nose
the only brain that matters now,

that space between snout
and the scent of the gar
more joined than cloven,
less deep than richly layered over.

Standing on the Back Porch

Standing on the back porch
of yet another house,
I hit Franklin over the head
with an orange-crate.
It made a funny, purple sound,
and there was mother, materialized,
screaming that I'd
spilled out Franklin's brains.
Like dead weight then
I joined my brother,
searching.
But I found nothing—
because Franklin,
both hands flared like a cradlecap,
was holding himself in.

That night in bed
I showed Franklin
that spot just behind the hip
where I myself had been hit, I said,
but by a German tank.
He felt it with the same fingers
that he had used to hold his brains in,
and that particular time,
because of something moving
deep inside the marrow, I charged him nothing.

Mother Said She Was Glad Now

Mother said she was glad now
that we hadn't bought that new rug
for the living-room,
because father would have worn
a path there
with his infernal pacing—
back and forth all night all week,
holding the bad hand in the good,
staring down and through the place
where two of his fingers used to be.
They had been sheared off in a pulley,
had dropped then into a bucket
of 10-weight motoroil.

Father put them into a mayonnaise jar
filled with formaldehyde.
He said, *And that's just the beginning.*
Work for the county long enough, he said,
and sooner or later
it'll have you
strung out on a shelf
like a classroom:
from elbow to bunghole,
father said,
from here all the way to there,
he said,
and then some.

Beginning Then Myself for the First
Authentic Time to Die, I Go on Dying

Only moments before I heard my brother
calling out for help
I saw a baby bullsnake
pause in a tuft of shadow cast by bunchgrass,
a sign, maybe, a bad sign, probably,
and sure enough the water in the sandpit
darkened and my brother's blood
trailed him brightly out of the water,

the bulk of my brother's long young body
itself trailing the hands of the one
who I think to this day saved him.
You must understand, first,
that at the bottom of the roadside pit
lay an ancient Hudson that
for whatever cockeyed reason
plowed through a curbing of gravel

and sailed no doubt like the torso
of a bright blue gamebird
smack into the center of the pit.
Understand that the young driver survived,
that his steady beside him did not,
that for all those years her long hair
in our dreams tugged (more blonde than sinister)
at the scalp that in the front seat

how many fathoms down
lay in the lap of a different lover.
Who in his right mind would want anything

further to do with such a car?
Holding our breaths to the edge
of bursting, our eyes wide,
we scavenged its hulk inside and out,
dashboard and glovebox,

gearknob and clutch, and it was
Sorry Burman's boy, L.C.,
who held the record for time spent sitting
buoyantly behind the wheel, who drove that
buggy of death, he said, round trip
to Medicine Lodge—the hulk meanwhile,
and before and after,
settling itself to its axles

in the sand. And meanwhile too
my brother's right foot pumping blood,
L.C. (the L for Leroy) saying artery, artery,
thumb and finger of one hand
circling my brother's lower leg,
thumb and finger pressing now, now
releasing. Understand that hereafter
the dream thickens: the girl's blonde hair

less blonde, now more sinister
rising and rising in water darkened
by my brother's blood,
the boy behind the wheel
having smashed the glass
to leave the shard
that disguised as moss
will draw the blood

to darken once and for all
all memory of water. Understand:
not even L.C.'s thumb and finger
circling my brother's leg, pressing now,
now releasing, can purge the dream.
Nor old Montzingo, our doctor,
the heft of his deep liquid voice
settling cool and antiseptic

into the large dark eye of the victim.
O understand just this:
beginning then myself for the first
authentic time to die
I go on dying. Was it for all of us
the driver lost control of the Hudson,
the girl's hand warm to orange to hot
against the inside of his thigh?

My brother, tough little mudcat,
meanwhile heals,
lives to swim his tough immortal fins
deep into another and yet another
flat southcentral Kansas summer.
Well, he always did have (so his mother said)
more guts than common sense,
Franklin, my brother. Down, down

he goes, deep breath swallowed, eyes wide,
hands at the ends of long arms
parting water. And I in the bubble
of his slow narrow wake
wild in the wreckage of our little years
to know forever and a day at least
the fact of one surviving
one another.

Taking the Milk to Grandmother

Not the milk, but the color of milk:
first snow unblemished in a bottle.
Not the bottle, but the feel of bottle
hard and cool against the curling
of a small boy's hand.

On the way, the bottle cradled
in my left arm,
I stop to watch old man Thornton's minks
rising on their hind legs in their cages
watching me.

Not the mink, but the smell of mink,
small manure that trails me down the alley
until, dissembled and sweet,
it becomes the girl the big boys in the bathroom
unzip themselves and over arcs of urine

talk about: Virginia Mae, downright pretty
if she'd lose a little weight,
who eats like a horse and screws like a mink—
not sex, but the heft of sex,
the motion and the smell of sex,

old man Thornton's minks in darkness
repeating themselves, the draw I descend
to begin that final leg to grandmother's house
downhill repeating itself, to the tracks and beyond,
footsteps, my own, repeating and repeating themselves,

until they carry me onto the back porch
where the screendoor opens
and grandmother wide as a monument
fills the space and in both hands takes the milk
and invites me in for an oatmeal cookie

and the last of the milk from yesterday's bottle,
which rinsing and drying (her apron as towel,
the bluebells on her apron as towel:
not the bluebell, but the damp of bluebell
in the gnarl of hand that is grandmother)

she gives to me, bending gives to me,
with it a kiss that is the breath
of milk and cheese, the ancient aftermath of sex.
Kiss. Kiss. Kiss is the sound the act makes,
sex the mink that with its small manure

defines Virginia Mae. Halfway home
I toss the bottle into the air end over end.
At the end of the alley the milkcow grazes:
not the cow, but the ripening of cow,
day into day the ripening of udder

into the ripening of tit,
milk then into the pail and into the bottle
that hard and cool against the curling of a small
boy's hand finds its way into the hands of grandmother.

Tit. Not tit, but the sound of tit,
an empty bottle that having descended
end over end
from the height of its grand ascension
strikes the hand.

That Voice From a Brain Evolved to Dream

—for Loren Eiseley

We go into the hand-dug cave, my brother and I,
on our bellies down the slope of a tunnel
whose roof like the roof of the cave itself
sags with the criss-cross of pine and lath,
tarpaper and feedsack covered thickly with dirt
hauled up and out from the hole
where now with a match to the wick of a candle
we learn the meaning of secret, the truth of space.

The candle flickering
flickers my brother's face.
We have little to say:
the thrill of the cave has reduced us,
our open mouths the mouths of those first two carp
who amazed themselves by journeying just one step more
beyond that other step they took how many miles ago
away from water.

Damp the walls, after an early-morning rain
now seeping. Into a puddle my brother, barefoot,
works his toes. By the time the candle has spent itself,
my brother's feet, up to the ankles, up almost
to the high cuffs on his overalls,
are lost in ooze.

Earth, dark earth, is at the nose.
If we could see we might see
fingers scraping clay, inventing claws.
We speak, when at last we speak,

the croak of single syllables.

How long must we linger in this cave today,
my brother and I? Day into night,
night into long moist day, the thrill of the cave
reducing us on and on,
until the sound of a voice from a brain
evolved to dream
urges us to the flap at the top of the incline:

lord, you should see my little brother
with his snout
push through the flap,
should see him raising himself to his knees,
dirty little beautiful little lizard
stretching mightily to find its legs
in the Kansas sunshine.

We look around, oxygen tart as ginger on the tongue.
A hawk in the high blue sky is circling.
Except for the bird, we are alone —
that voice from a brain evolved to dream

                                        being
the warm soft indulgence of our own.

Rushing the Season

Early March. Grandmother,
rushing the season,
wants to see for herself again
her burial plot (did its boundaries
come through the winter intact? are the names
on the gray-to-white granite missing?)
and one more time again
in my green Ford coupe
I take her.

I don't want to. Jesus,
grandmother, what's the point?
I think, Thank God there's nobody here
to watch us: me beside my green Ford coupe,
one hand smooth
against a swell protective layer
of liquid wax,
grandmother in her wide rosy-beige coat
placing a potted geranium
just this side of the headstone.
When she bends over
I can see where her brown cotton hose end
and the flesh of her white heavy German thighs
begins. Christ, if there was anybody here
wouldn't it be embarrassing.
But it's too early for the new lime growth
that will mark another milestone
on the limbs of the younger cedars,
too soon even for a fresh start of leaves
on the Chinese elms.
Just me and grandmother, Anna,

rushing the season,
placing a geranium above where grandfather
already is, where grandmother
is, she'll tell me later,
about to be.

There is as always, in spite of the sunshine,
a bone-chilling wind bearing down
from the north, and as always
I am freezing my ass to death
in my shirtsleeves. Grandmother,
satisfied at last with the tilt of the geranium,
straightens herself,
stands then with her short arms folded
as if to memorize again the underside
as well as the top
of the scene.

You ever been in a small-town cemetery
like that, with an old woman, alone?
One thing you can count on:
there will be a couple of kingbirds
close by, screaming up a storm.
And though it is never very long
before grandmother returns to the car,
already beside her I am another full head taller.
It is my opinion, for whatever it's worth,
that my grandmother in some strange old-woman way
loves me. I tell her to take her time.
Why not? By now my ass is solid ice.
I am opening the door.

In the Treehouse with Franklin

In the treehouse with Franklin
I listen to the pulse of the wood,
song of the hard rock maple,
Franklin beside me mashing an ear
against the largest of the limbs
we hammered all day
blue thumbs into.

At what age was it precisely
that Franklin came at last
to believe in the music of wood?
After the storm, after the flash
that will send this tree,
this treehouse of unpainted pine,
to oblivion,
it is Franklin who with a handsaw
will preserve a length of the limb
that at dusk that day, that hour, that instant,
he grew into.

Whittle and sand, sand and polish,
the hand that holds the wood
an almighty extension,
grain of the hard rock maple
rising to a hard rock sheen.

It is dusk of a long day in August.
In this house of pine and of hot collapse
the will of the hand that held the wood
holds on:
brother, in this gathering darkness,

leaves unmoving,
wing of a dove slanted white
in the shaft of a sturgeon moon,
you are rising to join me,
rung by rung
by rung by rung
to join me,
to sit with me here in this gathering darkness
together
to hear the song.

Whatever Is Elevated and Pure, Precisely on Key

In that house we called the R & M Café
I awoke each morning to the sound of Frankie Laine,
the bedroom where I slept curled beside my brother
a thin wall's distance from the nickelodeon.
And my own heart began to know ever so gently
what the wild goose knows, the double edge of its truth
a sanctum of sound, long and sweet and liquid and always
        tenor.

In the mixed chorus at the high school Glen J. Biberstein
sang with his eyes closed, his chin high,
the tip of his nose pointed at a warp of ceiling
above the transom. *Tenebra factae sunt,*
the words lofty and mysterious among the mouths
of so many Baptists and Pentecosts and United Brethren.
Whatever is elevated and pure, precisely on key,
Mr. LaVoie, the music teacher, said, is somehow holy,
is enough almost sometimes to see us through.

So do we sell the café and move to the promise
of higher ground? Mother, beside a vat of French fries
not yet accounted for, shifts the weight of her sweet
heavy heart from one foot to another. Father
with his floating kidney floats from counter
to booth to table, the padding of his footsteps
yes to no to yes with indecision.

At the controls of the pinball machine the paperboy
is taking a break. Pete Catlin like a virtuoso
begins to play the keyboard of the nickelodeon.
Omar Boland, retired from the hatchery, explains

the ins and the outs of coccidiosis. And
the sound of Frankie Laine rises high and clean
to a layer of ten-year grease against the ceiling.
Glen J. meanwhile is somewhere distant and probably
alone, rehearsing. Wild goose, brother goose, which
is best: the foot, wandering? the heart, at rest?

On the Road, Sunday, March 6, 1977

Supper at Marlo's Café
in Watertown, South Dakota:
two strips of bacon
on a hamburger patty
rife with cheese,
all welded snug as rivets
to an unburned bun.

For two bits the jukebox
will do its best
to keep your mind
off your French fries:
O dropkick me, Jesus,
through the goalposts of life!

A hundred miles, more or less,
to Aberdeen,
where from an unscreened window
near the top of the Ward Hotel
the points of a deserted Spur Lounge
look like the Seven Heavenly Sisters
dressed fit to kill.

In front of the OK Tire Store
a trucker pullchains his air horn
until all of the geese
this side of the Badlands
take up the song.

Inside Room 500 the radiator
does a small unobtrusive dance,

melting the last of the snow on Channel 3.

The bedsheets smell of starch.
There is nothing any longer left to do
or undo.

So I think of my family,
of my wife,
of the four children, one by one,
of the first grandchild,
now 3.5 days old,
out of the hospital and at home now,
and at the edge of sleep
I see her guileless breath usurp the cracks
of her white thin-slatted crib,
shaping then its charge
to outfox the keyhole:

on then beyond the melodic heft
of Marlo's Café
in Watertown, South Dakota,
to the Ward Hotel in Aberdeen,
to Room 500,
to the bed where at the edge of sleep
I welcome it to breathe it in
to breathe it out again
and on and on.

O Michelle!
O infant far from everything but home!
On our long descent to sleep
we are all of us one family, after all,
and all alone.

Trying to Love You in These Words

—for Eloise,
after thirty years

Trying to love you in these words
I choose these words:
palm of the hand,
small of the back,
ankle, eye.
Out of the water now
we reach unfinished arms

to reach each other. O dreamer,
just for this moment
suspend the dream:
palm of the hand,
small of the back,
ankle, eye,

all around them nothing
but the grim sweet obstacle
of air.
With these words
I just this moment

part that air,
palm of my hand
at the small of your back,
word *ankle*, word *eye*

becoming ankle and eye as
out of the water now,

deep water now,

in the wash of you,
ankle to eye,

I am going under.

Last Summer and the One Before

Father holds the melon
out from his buckle
as if a green container
about to christen the bow
of a new world. When the fruit
strikes the ground
I hear the meaning of broken.
With our hands
we scoop the heart crimson and sweet
into our mouths.
I spit a black seed
into a yellowing of yardlight,
turn to see a full moon
rising above the wheatfield
like the start of a new life.

Who knows why the tractor
slipped out of gear,
why its owner didn't look up
from his work at the sicklebar
sooner. I go to the funeral in a shirt
so stiff at the neck I am lost to say
who sat behind me.
Not even the fan overhead
can whirl away the heat
previewing hades, and Rock of Ages
drags like a four-bottom plow
choked time and again
with stubble. Heavens to Betsy, uncle says,
don't you know hardly
anything at all? Life is the learning of

which is which, the fixed law
or the sliding rule,
meaning, I guess, that because
I drink the last full dipper
I must take the bucket alone to be replenished
back to the deepening well.

Cycle

From the wrecks of five
I put together one
bicycle,
then smooth and paint it
an early-summer
green.

Mother and father
meanwhile call
each other
words that bring
the leaves down,
snow then so
beautifully deep
I freeze to death
only moments away
from the back-porch
screendoor.

I awaken
to the burden
of a heavy wind,
beyond a field of glass
tree limbs like lanky arms
testing the air
for miracles.
When at last
the world tilts
it tilts in our
favor.

The spring sun
hits the handlebars
with a brilliance
that very nearly
blinds. In the trees
birds are letting loose
with birdtalk so pure
that buds in spite
of some of us are
trying it once
more.

1943

I have measles
the size of those splotches
on the backs of my grandfather's hands.
My uncle says, The sun don't shine
on the same dog's ass
all the time. Did I know that already?

I know it now. And more:
that once in a while the sun
for all its magnitude
don't shine on some dogs' asses
ever at all.

The war meanwhile does not
end. The Philippines. Iwo Jima. Saipan.
I assault my own malady
with a frontal dose
of patience, or try to. Be rowdy, uncle says,
and the limbs on the family tree
might be doomed to extinction.

I like my uncle, who is 4-F
and ashamed almost to the death, he says,
that he is. Flat feet
and a floating kidney,
not to mention the asthma.
He buys a war bond every week,
comes home holding it
like a sweet laceration
against the wheezing in his barrel chest.
If he was in battle, he says,

he'd loose his right flat foot
against the retreating nether eye
of an entire Axis battalion.

I knew that already. Yet
when our town's first body comes home
my uncle is not much tougher
than the tissue he uses to swell his nose on.
It's the first time in all my days
I have seen a grown man cry. Is it that,
or the relentless drizzle at the cemetery?
When the rifles explode
I am the only urchin who does not snake swiftly
into the smoky craters
of spent shells. And besides,
my uncle's hand is a cradlecap
squeezing to a pulp my new-mowed hair. You
and your measles, he says, though
I am healthy now, though
I am better than new. You and your
goddam measles.

The Price of Admission

Yes, and I'd have it too,
if Eldon Barker hadn't gotten there first—
to Fanny Young's, I mean,
where he must have impressed her
with his fancy new gasoline mower,
so that now he has the money
and I don't. Hell,
I can turn all of my pockets inside-out
and have nothing to show
but my knife and maybe a lintball.

Now everywhere I go,
no matter how fast I go there,
Barker has been there before me,
all the old widows' lawns all over town
mowed smooth as a haircut,
my own mower, an outdated blue-handled pusher,
collecting cobwebs and rust
in the lean-to next to the house.

As if that isn't enough,
Betty Grable in about six hours
will be singing and dancing in a new one,
Coney Island, and I don't have
so much as the price of admission. As if
that isn't enough, the Cards are losing
to the Yankees, damn that Musial
all the way to Wednesday. Where is the man's
big bat when we need it?

As if. . .
Mom and dad have stepped up their quarreling,
words giving way last night
to something more palpable.
There was blood on the steering wheel.
Maybe they did it driving,
up one block and down another,
or maybe around and around the same block,
not wanting to do it in the house
in front of the kids,
but on the other hand
not bothering to clean up the mess. Or

            maybe they went somewhere and parked,
to the catalpa grove north of town, say,
and maybe they fully intended
to talk things through, to iron out
once and for all
all of those nasty wrinkles,
maybe even to kiss and make up,
maybe to touch each other
easily here and over here,
and maybe the words went well for a while,
until something slipped quick and sour
from somebody's lips,
and all hell broke loose—who knows?

I know this much:
the absence of money is a sore
that cannot heal.
All morning I combed this one-horse town
for scrap iron, Barker's mower in my ear
like a P-51. The absence of money

leads to the absence of Betty Grable:
and if a tube in this old radio
should fail,
the World Series for ages hence
would go up in smoke.

The absence. . .
It's what leads to blood the color of liver
on the steering wheel.

Barker of course is the one to be
overtaken: after the game
I slash my Barlow as if a machete
into a high density of cobwebs,
oil the blades and the flat cutting edge
and take my pusher into the thick falling
leaves of confrontation.
At this point I do not know
that the Cards will lose the Series,

four games to one,
that there isn't enough scrap iron
in all of God's creation (in spite
of the cloud that will rain on Hiroshima)
to bring back Clara Mackey's son,
that Betty Grable's legs will loosen first
their grip on Harry James,
next on living,
that mom and dad will make it, after all, each
alone. I am pushing an outdated blue-handled mower
at a dangerous speed
in the general direction of everybody's lawn.

George Eat Old Gray Rat at Pappy's House Yesterday

—for David Lee

It's the crutch I lean upon
to spell geography,
but I lose the spelldown anyway,
going under on occurrence.
Donna Grace Davis, only daughter
of the superintendent,
wins.

Grandmother used her arthritic cane to show me
what to pick up and where to place it,
garden hose, rake, hoe, flowerpot,
the rocker with its cushions
dank from the wind that rising and rising
will slap the rain like buckshot
against the windows. It is not the storm
she fears, it is the threat of dying
out of place. Who was it that said
Be in advance of all parting?

Now the garden hose
hangs in its perfect loops
from a spike in the carless garage,
the rake just here, the hoe there,
the petunias in their delicate bodies
high and dry in the kitchen. Grandmother
could not be happier, more at ease.
We will pop a tub of corn and play Parcheesi
until, sure enough, not long after
I know the storm will never end

the storm will end, and grandmother's arm
like a length of weathered wood
will steady me out of my clothes
and into the bedroom, where into a featherbed

I'll fall like heaviness
dropped from a great height, memory
undermining that moment between the flicker
and the dream, how back at my desk
I held a new yellow pencil in both hands,
how when I determined
what I thought to be its exact center
I pressed it between my thumbs,
snapping forever until the next occurrence
the proud Ticonderoga
of its spine.

At Shannon's Creek, Early August

This is the baptism I am not prepared for,
the one that in a moment of no reflection
I agreed to,
and now it is almost time.

We are in Shannon's pasture,
Shannon's Herefords nearby, their bellies
heavy with Shannon's buffalo grass,
water from Shannon's creek cooling their cuds,
and we are naked.

And where our clothes were
we are white, amazingly so,
the obese minister with his round face
and his testicles too small to matter,
and Oscar Koeppen out of his wheelchair
moving under his own steam
like a crooked crab
toward the water.

And I am white, too, that fishbelly white
I wouldn't want my date for the life of me to see,
me here because I agreed to be,
because Oscar in a note said he would do it
if I would, that he hoped I would.
He is an old man of no age,
his mouth no less twisted than his limbs,
his larynx unable to turn sound
into what we others know as sense.

They say it was God who made the heavens and the earth,
pasture and water
and the Herefords that standing nearby
watch us.
And made the preacher, too,
with me his nearest child, and Oscar,
who accepting the awful wrath of crookedness
asked that this ceremony not be done
in church, where those who do not understand
might smile their perfect lips,
but here in Shannon's creek,
and what I believe is this, that Oscar Koeppen
in his own distended way
believes.

And what I believe is that the preacher,
reciting the word, handling first Oscar, then me,
affirms for himself—as if a sanctification—
what is and what might have been.

And what I believe is that the waterhole we find
to be immersed in
filled before the first agreement,
and that after Oscar's bones are straightened
to fit his box of undetermined pine,
and the preacher with his folded hands
has lost that lust to touch his pitiful sac
to some consenter's skin,
and after age on age the boy
accepts the date who age on age
accepted him—

the waterhole will yet be filling.

The Mad Farmer Shuts Himself
Inside His Silo to Sing Away the Storm

—for and after Wendell Berry

Because the silo is round
each note is round,
each note eternity in a nutshell,
and knowing this the mad farmer
knows also that his song can never be lost,
never exhausted, never indefinitely contained,
until the storm relents,
until the door left open permits them
freedom

and they will go then inevitable as seed
to the four great corners of the universe,
there to put themselves together over and over,
becoming over and over the song
that now at the height of the storm
the mad farmer hat in his hand
stands singing:

O la and la and earth and water and wind,
sunlight and shadow,
la and la and hands deep into the soil,
and work and love,
and the greatest of these is work
and love and hands, la and la and
the immaculate equation of knowhow
and concern

until the silo spins with the mad farmer's song,

until the storm with its thunder and lightning
joins in,
la and la and crack and rumble,
and knowing these, and the fathers
and the mothers and the children of these,
the mad farmer hat yet dripping in his hand
invents a final verse, releasing each word
with its attendant note whole as faith

into the space that waits to be more than itself
when the storm relents
and the sun does its own savage work
and the harvest behold! is in.

Watercolor: The Door

Its charm is a low whisper
somewhere between a man's sound
and a woman's,
and you move toward it
with all the caution of age,
knowing how edges sometimes
shift their sudden perspectives
to disengage you.

The amazing thing
is that this old thing
is indeed so old,
done by one of the children,
mounted and framed then
by a pride too inclusive for borders.
The amazing thing
is that the colors—pastels,
except for the whorl of red,
as if a bloodprint, on the
knob—remain as they were
the hour, the moment
you first set eyes upon them.
On the overhead a small surplus
of aqua, yet running.
And in a lower corner, blocked,
almost as if a welcome,
        WATERCOLOR:
        THE DOOR.

You cannot open it
to move on to another life
until it dries,
and it never dries.

Testament

I carry it in my left breast pocket
to keep me safe from those sudden splatterings
no one fully understands. Love thy neighbor
hits me with the force of a dum-dum.
I do a James Cagney death,
then flat on my back
I open my eyes and wink
and point at the chapter and the verse
that saved me. My neighbor,
that incorrigible ass, seems almost human,
bending over me like a bewildered medic,
his life a bad account he can't apparently
stop compiling.

When I regain the strength I never lost
I substitute a .50-caliber for the testament,
an act that one might call, in search
of something dense, the gift of prophecy. Because
tonight a wild evangelist
will hurl his Bible like a shot
in the specific direction of my heart,
and thanks to the tough and phallic casing
I'll live to tell it,
how the good Lord loves his children
with a vengeance,
how the point of anything
worth punishment forever
rings hollow.

Independent

1.
A recent issue of the hometown paper
turns bloodhound to sniff me out,
and I read that the church
where I learned to have no other gods
before it
has merged with a larger denomination,
the stuccoed building, big as a poor boy's
castle, sold then to the Baptists,
and quick as a miracle I mix myself a drink.

2.
Jesus. The world is a quaint and ornery place,
isn't it? In the basement during prayer meeting
I used my Scofield Bible to cover my hand
holding hers. Later, in the haymow,
we tied forbearance to necessity
with a length of grocery twine
born to break. Surely you know what I mean.
This must have been what Adam and Eve did,
having blown a kiss goodbye to Eden.

But Baptists. Holy smoke. They too
fornicate, I know, but always after the act
it shows, too much grease on an axle
turning nowhere. Now they move and breathe
and have their being in that place
where I learned never to judge
unless the moment demands it,
and sitting a polished pew as if a pony

I find myself beside her,
reading between the lines of the hymnal
the message of multiplication
ever after. O
life is a quaint and ornery movement,
isn't it?

3.
The football team meanwhile has beat the daylights
out of the Sharon Bobcats—Sharon, for the Lord's sake,
that hotbed of Catholics where one Saturday night
I saw a perfectly swell fistfight,
the principals equally naked to the waist,
equally drunk,
the sound their fists made
against their equally beautiful bodies
reaching all the way to the lowest bolgia
of the stomach.
But Baptists? I am surprised at my own
astonishment,
I who have not subscribed to the *Independent*
for thirty years, I who haven't
darkened a church door in a month of Sundays,
but apparently I have not yet given up
all the ghosts, and I mix another drink
at the thought of Baptists twitching and jerking
in the church where I learned to endure my neighbor,
and I swear I can't help it, I feel betrayed,
what little hair I have to run a hand through
clipped close by someone else's hand
while I lay sleeping.

4.

And there were bums in those days, tramps,
and while the churchfolk extemporized
and worked at finding God
with wet fingers
against the gossamer leaves of Holy Scripture
my mother took them in and gave them
mush and Ovaltine
and wrapped the little wool we had to spare
around their necks and sent them off with words
that must have returned to them a hundredfold
as they sat near the Santa Fe tracks
hunched over a dirtbowl of cinders, Lord,
can you hear what I'm saying? The church
where I learned that the meek shall inherit
what's left of the earth
has been sold like something tangible
to the Baptists,

and I would therefore have another drink,
during which I'll trust my fingers
to find hers somewhere
under Ecclesiastes, that thrill meanwhile
of those beautiful bodies
clashing,
the flattened nose, the blood, the white eye
wild in the hold of its socket,
the bad to the good news being delivered
forever and a day somehow
by whatever institutional animal
slouching home.

Lovers

I look out the front-room window
to see a pair of youngsters
holding hands at the bus stop.

I run my fingertips
along the arms of the recliner,
peachfuzz delicate as memory.

And I tell myself that I know
how they feel, touch
synonymous with shiver, blood
beyond the touch
hot and irreversible.

And so it is that they are kissing
when the bus arrives,
and without parting
they wave it on.

In this shy neighborhood
another bus will not be along
for an hour. I want
to invite them in,
give them the universal key
to the secret room.

The girl in the book I am reading
has black hair, too,
black and straight,
and the bold words on the page
tell me that in the darkness

her face is a white oval
in a framework of stars.

When I look up, the lovers
are gone.
The girl with the oval face
invites me in,
gives me the universal key
to the secret room.
When I look up, the lovers
because I say so
have returned.

Cave

Not the one in the southwest corner of the backyard
under the stunted elm,
whose roots my brother and I chopped away at
hour after hour into the dusks
of interminable days,
not the hole in the dark earth
that evolved in spite of our mother's dark
predictions, the hole whose sides
we smoothed with a borrowed spade
until the soil shone bright
and as hard as porcelain,
and not the cover of lath and cardboard
and gunny sack and new-turned earth,
swaybacked and finally tight enough
to deny most light,
but the bedroom where all of us slept
through the long nights of August
while a Kansas moon took its shape
through a butterfly snag in the windowblind.

These hands that helped to dig the backyard cave
are yet my hands, this drink in them
cool to the touch, cool and as damp
as the backyard cave my brother and I,
with candle and matches,
first crawled into, lowering carefully
the lid to the secret entrance, on our bellies
following the beam of the flashlight
down the short slope of tunnel
into the cool damp hole. And the candle,
placed into a recess in the south wall,

how it caught with the third kitchen match,
flickering then, then gasping,
and my brother and I settling our backs
against the cool damp earth and sighing,
as if to say This is it. This is the place
where not even Sunday school can reach us.

I would have another drink, the effluvium
of whiskey distinct as my mother's breath,
her face near mine,
her heavy form bending over me to tell me
Drink: your croup is loosening, but
it's keeping your father awake. And
what of your own voice earlier that night, mother,
and of father's responding,
shouting in whispers that money is the god
we live to believe in but cannot lay our
hands on, the whispering
intense to the point of knives,
made more intense by my brother's easy breathing,
my sister's face in the snag of moonlight
no more disturbed than a saucer
of untouched cream.

Ancient history is what you can choose
not to remember. All else is a gathering
into the present, and that in turn a gathering.
Time to get ready for Sunday school, mother says,
her body bent, her face close to mine.
It is the kind of face that at night, lying
beside my father, wants to know
just where in the name of Jesus Christ
the money for the children's winter clothes

is supposed to come from. Faith
is the victory, the minister says, and
when we pray I don't, nor does Eileen,
our eyes meeting deeply and squarely
until the praying says Amen.

In the damp of the backyard cave,
the candle gasping,
I tell my little brother something
about her. On his tongue the word Tit
is the pearl of redemption. I tell him
more than I know. His face in the
flicker of candlelight is the face of an angel.
This is not the true cave, understand,
this is the hole in the southwest corner
of the backyard,
the jut of an elmroot the nail I hang my hat on.
He wants to know if what I have learned
will ever happen to him. Faith
is the victory, I say. I say Amen.

In the true cave the August nights
do not relent, snag of moonlight
on my sister's face, my brother so evenly
breathing. I would have another drink.
When the candle goes out, and the last match
fails to flame, my brother and I
talk softly in the darkness,
threats of God and of money
as if the trailing edges of a vast
but dissipating dream. Between her legs,
I tell him, already are traces of hair.
And I remember the sense of awe

that rode on his intake of air,
the palpable sound of his laughter. While
in the bedroom the whispering
slowed time's motion. The bedroom,
the true cave, not the backyard hole
with its spent candle, its silence,
the words from my brother and me
suspended, but the room where all of us sleep
through the long nights of August
while a Kansas moon takes its shape
though a butterfly snag in the windowblind.

Drinking the Tin Cup Dry

Tin against the boy's lip,
cool water slaking the tongue,
and my father, the hired hand,
hip-deep in wheat in the bed
of the unpainted wagon,
shoveling.

Father,
I cannot drink deeply enough
to drink this tin cup dry.
With each effort the stubble
rotates to become the darkened soil
that having housed the seed
gives rise to another windless day,
and you are at it again,
sickle and chaff and the women
in their blue bandanas (I among them,
the incorrigible, the tagalong,
wanting to inhale the world)
bringing bread and purple grapes
and lunch-meat. And you, father,
the hired hand, stopping for nothing,
not for sympathy, least of all for hunger,
until the last of the kernels from the combine
lies dutifully spread.

Father,
all of this aches to be ancient history.
But the tin cup
finds its way into my hand
at the oddest hour, the party

rampant with the thighs of city girls
and the tinkling of ice in bourbon,
and there is nothing for it
but to lift and drink:

my face
in the cool water, beyond it
you in the wagonbed
up to that place that did its work
to place me here
breathing the death of us all
in the midst of such plentiful grain.

Riding My Bicycle
Without Hands Down Huntington Street

the secret children
has something to do with the circling
something to do with heft and with momentum
something to do with the urge
to look back over the right shoulder
only of ancient memory

which means that if virginia mae brown
could see me now she most certainly
would repent that most wretched
of all denunciations

don't look to walk me home
after choir wednesday nights
and don't come sniffing and ogling
into the kitchen for me
billy you creep for you
I have snapped my last bean

the poor child did not realize
the extent to which at forty-six
I should come to master this bicycle

I keep one eye on the front wheel
the other on a dumptruck
in my rear-view mirror
bearing down

with arms fully extended
I bless the grass the trees

the delicate bursts of flag and birdsong

I am giddy and far gone with the season
inebriate of place
of the breeze that makes a touchstone
of the eyes
the face

God is a handlebar in the sun
I give one hand to an old woman
dying on her front lawn
she accepts it kisses it revives
cackles hallelujah all the way to kingdom come

(what was it anyway I rode away
to be away from)

I give the other to the truck
which with a stub I christen the virgin brown
to its heft to its momentum
to spoke and wheel
like the color of midday in nebraska
along huntington street in lincoln in nebraska
going around going down and around and around

Out-and-Down Pattern

—for John

My young son pushes a football into my stomach
and tells me that he is going to run
an out-and-down pattern,
and before I can check the signals
already he is half way across the front lawn,
approaching the year-old mountain ash,
and I turn the football slowly in my hands,
my fingers like tentacles
exploring the seams,
searching out the lacing,
and by the time I have the hands positioned
just so against the grain-tight leather,
he has made his cut downfield
and is now well beyond the mountain ash,
approaching the linden,
and I pump my arm once, then once again,
and let fire.

The ball in a high arc
rises up and out and over the linden,
up and out and over the figure
that now has crossed the street,
that now is all the way to Leighton Avenue,
now far beyond,
the arms outstretched,
the head as I remember it
turned back, as I remember it
the small voice calling.

And the ball at the height of its high arc
begins now to drift,
to float as if weightless
atop the streetlights and trees,
becoming at last that first bright star in the west.

Late into an early morning
I stand on the front porch,
looking into my hands.

My son is gone.

The berries on the mountain ash
are bursting red this year,
and on the linden
blossoms spread like children.

My Love for All Things Warm and Breathing

I have seldom loved more than one thing at a time,
yet this morning I feel myself expanding, each
part of me soft and glandular, and under my skin
is room enough now for the loving of many things,
and all of them at once, these students especially,
not only the girl in the yellow sweater, whose
name, Laura Buxton, is somehow the girl herself,
Laura for the coy green mellowing eyes, Buxton
for all the rest, but also the simple girl in blue
in the back row, her mouth sad beyond all reasonable
inducements, and the boy with the weight problem,
his teeth at work even now on his lower lip, and
the grand profusion of hair and nails and hands and
legs and tongues and thighs and fingertips and
wrists and throats, yes, of throats especially,
throats through which passes the breath that joins
the air that enters through these ancient windows,
that exits, that takes with it my own breath, inside
this room just now my love for all things warm and
breathing, that lifts it high to scatter it fine and
enormous into the trees and the grass, into the heat
beneath the earth beneath the stone, into the
boundless lust of all things bound but gathering.

Camping on the North Bank of the Platte

—for Harvey Potthoff

Early evening,
and the young people are wading the river,
becoming bold in its clear shallow currents,
their laughter hanging distinct and immobile

in the warm and windless air.
They will not be surprised when later
the storm blows in, slapping the tents,
no more surprised when just as suddenly

the storm moves on,
when night with its myriad stars
settles over their luminous bodies
like a weightless comforter.

They are in love
with the inevitability of joy.
When they sleep
they sleep the insolent sleep

of the stone. O Lord,
how the power of the absence of guile
might buy and sell this world!
Mother, grandfather, who was the first

to permit the dream its entrance
into the lizard's brain?
In our own sweet partial ways
we are immortal.

Christmas 1940

In the basement
of the church
our teacher shows
us how to manage
flannel, and soon
enough the pieces
come together:
camel and bright
star, wise man
and shepherd and
Mary beside a
slatted manger.

My part in the play
is to stand still,
my right hand steady-
ing a fresh-cut
length of catalpa.
Baby Jesus is a
large-faced doll
belonging to Velma
Jean's mother. It
was bought, Velma
Jean says her mother
said, at a great
price. Break it or
lose it, you don't
need to bother to
come home. I am
Joseph, but some-
how I am not

the father.

Santa Claus comes in
through a high win-
dow, bells jingling,
over his shoulder a
bedsheet filled to
overflowing. When
he falls we laugh,
and when we learn
next day that he had
cracked his collar-
bone, we laugh
even harder.

I hide my sack of
candy at a place
inside the barn
from which it van-
ishes overnight,
making its
goodness last
forever.

The Louvre

—for Gladys Lux

Today it's the Louvre. Yesterday
it was Chartres,
where the guide, having said
that the blues in the windows
could not be explained,
tried to explain them. And I remember
how blue was the bottle of Evening in Paris
I spent my last dime on,
how night after Saturday night
the lobes on my girlfriend's ears

drove me crazy. But that was yesterday,
at Chartres. Today it's the Louvre,
where Mona Lisa behind a doubled wall of glass
hangs motionless, defying gravity,
where the backs of the gleaners
bend forever into their harvest,
where man and woman recline together
as if unashamed,
their bodies so immediate
I touch mine. Yesterday, at Chartres,

after the tour and the Gothic singing,
I bought a pocket knife
with Chartres in gold on the handle,
one bright blade and a corkscrew. All
up and down my left index finger
I have scars to prove my love
of pocket knives,

how the dullest among them
can go in a blink to bone, how
my girlfriend held the bloody bandage

near her lips as if to kiss it. But
that was yesterday, at Chartres. Today
it's the Louvre,
where I stand with so many others, my wife
beside me, all of us wild to create ourselves
with the stroke of whatever brush
so that, created, we might begin
the formulation of another work,
all of us wild to deny
what cannot be denied,

our ashes given to ashes,
our dust to dust.

An Interlude for Morning

—for Phyllis Ernst

> If I had a thing to give you,
> I would tell you one more time
> that the world is always turning
> toward the morning.
>
> *—Gordon Bok*

And I would give you
that morning,
would have you rise
determinate
with the sun's
slow rising. Would
in the high sweet glow of morning
approach to catch from you
a portion of the morning's
overflowing.

Warm is the good earth struck
point-blank by the sun,
warm the good word
turning.

Grass newly-clipped
launches the back yard
into a slow roll of emerald
pasture, a robin
the size of a milkcow
grazing the blades. Lime
from the leaves on the cottonwood

heightens the lips. Now we
understand, don't we, our glasses
raised in a toast to the moment,
what ice is?

With these words,
and the breath of these words,
I give you that morning,
its heat within your body
brightening the beholder's eye.
With these words,
and the breath of these words,
I give you that morning,
and with it all those mornings
toward which evening cannot choose
but move, now
and for as long as
breath and word shall last,
and ever after.

The Day I Pedaled My Girlfriend
Betty Lou All the Way Around the Paper Route

was a warm day in August of forty-five,
her name warm as the day,
her eyes no less dark than her hair,
her skin unblemished ivory. How

with one swipe of her own deft tongue
her red lips reddened. Shall I mention
the following, that her teeth were white
and immeasurably straight? They were.

From where she stood on the cracked sidewalk
in front of the drugstore
she called me, her words,
whatever they might have been,

wonderfully urgent.
I was pumping a purple Hawthorne bike,
its purple faded to a most delicate pastel.
Was it the color, or my motion astride it,

that commanded Betty Lou's dark eye?
In less time than it takes to remember
she was sitting sidesaddle
on the crossbar,

her ivory fingers clutching below the handles
as if they meant to stay there
for the duration. Clockwise
around the fringes of my small hometown

we circled, twin sacks
on either side of the Hawthorne
filled to overflowing
with the high black headlines of war.

And a week from now
the message of victory
with its sickening undertones
will start its murmur: A-bomb,

fallout, halflife, Hiroshima,
radiation, ground zero,
Nagasaki,
vocabulary sufficient

to stun the most highly fortified
of lexicons. Betty Lou meanwhile
wore a pleated skirt
green as those leaves on the catalpas,

and her tan blouse for all its cotton
could not entirely flatten
the points of her breasts. Clockwise
around the fringes of my small hometown

we circled, Betty Lou's thin legs
hanging lovely and lofty from the crossbar,
my pumping of the purple Hawthorne bike
stirring a breeze to send dark hair

flowing into my face, my mouth,
the mix of hair and of breath
that union that maybe believers mean

when they sing of how beautiful

heaven must be. So what do I remember?
That the movement clockwise
did not indefinitely
last. That

when I passed the back yard at Bullard's,
and my buddies at basketball
looked up and started to wave but didn't,
I did. That trying not to sweat

I felt the moisture coursing the spine
like a rivulet. That
when I crashed a paper through
Ruby Nelson's screendoor

Betty Lou's laughter,
out from the ivory palace of her mouth,
gave me the strength of more
than a hundred. That

I can hear the sound of that laughter yet,
eons beyond the lexicon embodying
A-bomb, fallout, halflife, Hiroshima,
radiation, ground zero,

Nagasaki. That the circle we finally finished
is never finished. That
the burned and wasted bodies of children,
though gone, are never gone.

Nebraska, Early March

The sun one hour from setting
distinguishes the landscape,
so red the barn,
so white the house,
each weathered board
so cleanly defined
on the slatted grainbin.
And the hay, each mound,
and the cattle, each calf
beside each cow so singular
against a slope of golden stubble,
and the stubble, each stalk,
and along the roadside the blue-
stem, each stem, and the fenceline,
each barb, and later the moon
through the window
washing our bodies, each
member, and your hair,
under my wildest touch each
indivisible strand.

The Night Joe Louis Went 21-0
By Dropping Tami Mauriello

I'm babysitting the Garlow boy,
  who is asleep now,
    and the fight is over,
      Louis having disposed of the challenger

at 2:09 of the opening round.
  Beside me on the porch swing
    sits the girl who knows more
      about my dreams than I do,

she is in them that much,
  her face so delicate that one
    right cross, one smart left jab
      would surely for all time spoil it,

and later I'll think how
  behind each great public event
    lies the small private one,
      how the small one, aware of the other,

measures itself against the lofty clamor
  until it's the private one that
    truly matters, that endures,
      almost as if the mind becomes convinced

that greatness is a ruse
  enabling smallness its breathing space,
    its down-home victory. Beside me my girl
      sits more than ever elegant and alert

because Mauriello, on his seat against the ropes,
   didn't, and her lips when I kiss them
     taste sweetly of the blood
      that isn't there. This night

is like a pod about to burst,
   an Indian-summer moon I swear
     within arm's reach beyond the trellis,
      the thumping of the dynamos

across town at the power plant
   as if the heartbeat of some God,
     almighty. Well, I knew all along the Bomber
      could not be whipped by a Bronx

bartender. I know, and my knowing
   adds a modicum of pride
     to the lust of the moment,
      Mauriello (I'll

read this tomorrow evening
   in the *Beacon*)
     weeping in his dressing-room,
      my girl and I so filled with whatever

weeping isn't
   we bite our tongues,
     I think to moderate the simple joy
      we'd otherwise indulge by crying.

You Have Lived Long Enough

You have lived long enough,
my mother tells me, when
wandering the halls of the
hospital you recognize each
face, each bone beyond each
face, and you have lived
long enough when you enter
each room to talk with each
face, your remembrances
cracking the mouths into
smiles that having lived long
enough you can trace to the
very roots—Aunt Vivian turn-
ing in triumph from her last
canned jar of plums, Uncle
Elmer pounding his cap against
the quaint immobile flywheel
of the tractor, another season
of planting thank god history.
And you have lived long enough
when the clean hard hallway
opens into that room where the
figure atop the whiteness is
yourself, and you do not
hesitate, you instead move
swiftly to your side and taking
your hand you start the story
that you have heard so many
many times yet cannot bring
yourself to tire of again.

Alone in the Sandhills of Sheridan County, Nebraska,
Standing Near the Grave of Mari Sandoz

She holds to her silence
as if death can be in fact
conclusive,
the lark meanwhile
from atop its perch of soapweed
stirring the warm June air
with the wand of its
high sudden song.

And this hillside, this delicate hogback,
how the late afternoon sun
shimmers its coarse green skin,
switchgrass and snakegrass and grama,
and above it all the wide bellies
of the Hereford and the Angus,
their calves beside them
red and black in the sunlight,
shimmering. And nearby the orchard,
Old Jules' apple and peach and plum trees
in a long thick line of open defiance,
beyond them the lowland meadow
sweet with impending hay,
and standing here
alone in the Sandhills
of Sheridan County, Nebraska,
near the grave of Mari Sandoz,
I would think something true
to match the perfect pitch of the lark,
against one of the barbs guarding the grave
would puncture myself to blood

to know and to keep it:
that I am here, alive
at this X my bootheel marks
in the earth of Sheridan County,
that above me the flash of the redwing
omens the blue sky now and tomorrow,
that I am as surely the object
of the kingbird's eye as I am
observer.

Until the gathering cirrus
begins to deplete the sun:
the throat of the pulley
when I push back the gravegate
whines. At my ankles
persist the burrs of lost uprisings,
lost intentions, lost loves,
while underfoot the grit
for all its eternal shifting
never moves.

After Breakfast With My Wife at the Hy-vee Diner

Softly on spring snow
I walk the twelve blocks
back to home,
an early-morning sun

about to burn its way
through a grey overhanging
of clouds. Where is the wind?
Where are the friends

who coughed their last
sweet bitter days
into a cauldron
sufficient beforehand to the brim?

Heavy with flakes
hang the limbs
of cedar and pine and linden,
cardinal on a green white bough.

This is the postcard
I would send. My wife
drove off to work,
where probably just now

she is speaking to youngsters
of their options,
preserving the baby
high among them. Meanwhile,

softly on spring snow
I walk the twelve blocks
back to home,
already on the lilacs

buds not far from bursting.
This is the postcard
I would send. Flake and cedar
and pine and linden,

cardinal on a green white bough.

Undressing by Lamplight

It's the uneven wick that does it,
a flickering that motions the body

already in motion—that,
and the slight sensation of kerosene

sending me to that spot behind the ear
I cannot easily come away from.

Look, monkeynuts, this is the tailend
of the twentieth century, you say,

megawatts enough to outdo the sun,
and I say Hush, I say

This was my grandparents' lamp,
how at the stroke of nightfall

grandfather took the fresh-toweled globe
from the hand of grandmother

to fit it then to the lampbase,
how in the lamplight the kitchen

mellowed, flickered and jumped,
this lamp is holy, I say, I say

Help me work the combination
of this infernal bra,

and we are undressing by lamplight,
undressing each other by lamplight,

and she is quiet now,
her eyes in the mirror

when she looks at me
like the eyes you sometimes come across

in the album you seldom open,
large and sepia and

dark with the lovely pain
of human understanding.

Easter Sunday

At the upright piano
Ernestine Trotter
sits in close and
heavy combat
with the choir: she
will play louder
than the choir
can sing, or
die trying.

The minister speaks
of that force
strong enough
to overcome the
immovable object.
He leans into the
pulpit, tipping it
forward until
somebody ohs.
When the juice is
passed I help my-
self to a double
portion.

Mother says that
for every container
there is the right
lid out there
somewhere. Yet
Ernestine I am told
will never know a

man. I watch her
pound the upright
in the general
direction of
oblivion, with each
stroke watch its
keyboard rise
as if the savior
we are singing about
again.

When I shake the
minister's hand
I shake limp
skin, take the
long steps down-
ward three at a
time. In my father's
house are only four
small rooms. I can-
not wait to shed
these unnatural
clothes, cannot wait
to go outside to
breathe where the
visible sun is.

Last of the Mohicans

—for Robert Hepburn

Each morning to start things off
Miss Yoder read to us
from a book so thick
I could not stop watching it,
read to us a story of capture,
and of flight and then of capture,
each morning her voice
going suddenly silent
at a moment when something awful
or maybe something terribly sweet
was about to happen,

and that's the way I have come
to live the other parts of my life,
my eyes on a book whose thickness
almost imperceptibly lessens,
she had read the story praise be! and alas!
so many times before,

and when one morning she wasn't there,
and thereafter never was,
how I expected her substitute to carry on,
though she never did,
that unfinished book
gone forever with Miss Yoder, herself a mystery
unfinished,
though day by day I have come
to realize the romantic extremities
of capture and of flight and then of capture,

of taking up what someone else

began, however incidental or deliberate,
however thick the volume we must alone conclude,
however thin.

Drifting

Because we cannot agree on a campsite
we continue to drift
until evening becomes a quarter-moon
spilling its necklace of stars
into the river. Carp
we saw earlier in daylight
come to us now
only on the fins
of their obscene sucking.

By now we should be
pitched and secure,
sitting warm by a campfire.
By now we should be
white teeth in a glow
of cottonwood, flash of eye
like a tilt of knife-
blade, cheekbones
radiant.

Downstream to starboard
a small square of light
breaks the darkness. Drifting,
I watch the light
become a window
of a distant farmhouse. Drifting,
I see a figure
moving inside the light,
a woman with long dark hair
wearing only a peach-colored slip.
How can I know this?

How can I know
that she is barefooted,
that she walks
on cool linoleum?
That after we have drifted
not only out of sight
but out of hearing

she will call me in?

The Others

Say that for a few moments
the brain reverts to become the lizard's,
and belly slick against the wet late-night grass
I hear the wind in the cottonwoods
singing an old hymn—

No matter. Lying belly-down on bunchgrass
wet and becoming wetter,
studying the orange in a deep bed of coals,
I hear the hymn, and Christ
I want to wake the others to hear it, too,

but I know that for a long time,
since before the clouds came in
to cover Venus,
the others have been asleep—tentflaps
secure, their breathing

beautifully heavy,
so I listen alone until the song is done,
then rising I walk to the river's edge
to hear the clapping of water
against the boats—

and because a thinning of clouds
expands the night
I move into the river to find the channel
to drift with my belly up with all the others

to catch the moon.

Abandoned Farmhouse

The figure in the abandoned farmhouse
moves slowly from room to room,
or would be moving, if there were in fact
a figure in the abandoned farmhouse.

The figure in the abandoned farmhouse,
a woman, moves tall and thin,
dressed only in a peach-colored slip,
and her bare feet more glide than walk

over the pine, the tongue, the groove,
over the patches of gray linoleum,
or would be gliding, if there were in fact
the pine, the tongue, the groove, the linoleum.

The pine, the tongue, the groove, the linoleum
are going, going, so that what
we chiefly see is an unpainted shell
inside of which the figure, tall and thin,

moves quietly from room to room,
moves by the light of the lamp
she holds chin-high before her
from room to room, into at last the kitchen.

From room to room, into at last the kitchen
the woman moves, or would be moving,
if there were in fact a farmhouse, in fact
a woman moving from room to room.

A woman moving from room to room
leaves the kitchen, or what would be a kitchen
if there were in fact a woman in a farmhouse,
abandoned, moving from room to room.

Abandoned, moving from room to room
she flows in silhouette until the lamp goes out,
and slowly then I go to bed to sleep
with the dream I cannot sleep without, this woman.

Wildwood, Early Autumn

—for Robert and Kate

This night above stars
sparkling the water
I sit alone at the pond's grassy edge
waiting for the line suddenly
to lose its slack,
channel catfish sleek as love
in a slant of mid-September moon.

And don't breathe a word of this
to anyone,
but what I'm hearing
is the music that came to me
so many nights ago
as I sat with the children's mother
on the front porch,
banjo and guitar and mandolin
taking turns in the hands
of the younger son, each chord
sweet as the amber wine
we sipped on,

and don't breathe a word of this
to anyone,
but the liquid in those tunes
must have found its way
to where the desert wants more
than anything else to bloom—Peaceful
Easy Feeling, Blackberry Blossom,
Autumn Leaves, Devil's Dream,

Comes a Time, Red-Haired Boy, Steam-
Powered Aeroplane—refreshing
each rib on each
up-and-coming spine,

and don't breathe a word of this
to anyone,
but the catch is this:
the melodies of earth
are never done: bullfrog,
thunderbird, a west wind
soughing through the saguaro—
and the fish I'll hook
but not possess,
its body, sleek as love,
this night forever at home
wherever home is.

In a Motel Room Somewhere in Western Nebraska

Through the large window
I can see clearly too many stars
to be clearly taken in.
So many nights in this distant life
have I tried to sort out to understand
what can neither be sorted out
nor understood.

As a Tenderfoot, for example,
I lay on a pallet of blanket and bunchgrass,
studying the stars, the campfire
a torrid and fallen moon, the scoutmaster
in his puptent snoring. I fell asleep at last
empty-handed, in the outer space of mind
reached no conclusion.

Now, on the smaller window across the room,
Nolan Ryan with the Rangers
registers his seventh career no-hitter.
At 44 he is proof that hero is something more
than concept—he is the star with flesh on its bone,
though the nerve-ends in his arm remain
elusive as the wink in the eye of Venus.

Later, as an Eagle, I ascended no higher
than the ground I stood on.
Except to wonder, as tonight I wonder,
about the backdrop that makes the glory possible:
the darkness beyond the stars,
the batter in the bottom of the beautiful ninth,
two gone, the count at two and two,
going, as they say the earth and heavens go,
around, around.

Dress

Once again my sister loses the battle,
meaning no store-bought dress,
meaning that again the old woman

here across the alley is sewing another outfit,
something not much fancier than a feedsack,
my sister standing on a wooden stepstool

while Mrs. Linshied kneels to adjust the hem,
my sister standing as tall as she can,
embarrassed and angry,

her green eyes looking straight ahead so hard
I look there, too,
but there isn't anything to see

except a purple flowing of pink wallpaper
until finally Mrs. Linshied finishes
and rises slowly to find her purse

to pay me, a few unused pins
sprouting from between her lips, old lips,
old porcupine, old hand

dipping into the purse for eighty cents,
three quarters and a nickel,
and taking the coins

I drop her paper on the seat of a rocking chair
which I kick when I turn to leave,
bad news all over the front page,

we're losing,
more Japs than bullets to kill them,
and that dumb old rocker

squeaking like something
small and cornered as
I shut the door.

Welcome to Carlos

Sunday Morning

Carlos learns things faster
than anyone in school.
Which is why he
goes to the Baptist church, he says,
because especially there
he can watch the natives being fools.
And he can carry that pleasure with him
back across the tracks—
not only the impression of flaying arms
and the whites of rolled-back eyes,
but those other pleasures, too, the ones
so totally apart from spite:
the sound of his own voice
swelling all those others,
the scent of April lilac
beneath the stain of an open window
that knows no line between
the day's long darkness
and the night.

Summer, 1944

Carlos' father is a gandydancer on the section crew
that works the rails between here and Kiowa
on the Panhandle Division
of the AT&SF. Carlos says
That's a mouthful.

On a shimmery day in July

we hopscotch the ties
on our way to a spring-fed hole,
javelins of bamboo over our shoulders
turning us into a brace of Huckleberry Finns.
When our patience has worn thin as a dime
Carlos sure enough catches a snapper
the size of Rhode Island. When he says
Turtle soup,
I spit my reaction
into the southcentral Kansas dust.

Carlos calls the turtle a dirty Nip,
with the short blade of his pocketknife
cuts all the way through its ropy neck.
On the way home, the whole kit and caboodle
in a gunnysack over his right shoulder,
Carlos balances himself and his prize on one rail
as if he knows something I might never know,
as if the universe were amateur
and he having paid his dues
had gone just now
professional.

Balls

The rumor is that Carlos' father
has taught himself to weld,
and with the knowledge
came a swift promotion. Carlos
shrugs. Now his father in overalls
does the family shopping
with a black igniter
swinging from the hammer loop.

He carries the bulging sack
home across the tracks
in silence,
one boot in front of the other,
and except for the igniter
swinging as if keeping time
this universe
unchanged.

And rumor has it that Carlos' father
is thinking of moving the family
to that open acreage just north
of the high school. Balls. You can
charge that one to the dust, Carlos says,
and let the rain settle it.

Convo

Sister Roberta comes to our school
to talk about the wondrous birth and
the limits of mercy and of life

everlasting, her full pink mouth
cattywampus,
one full click to starboard,

and I christen her Shirley Temple,
the Good Ship Lollipop sweet
as the Promised Land,

and I a sailor on a sea
whose ebb is the eye peripheral,
whose flow is tongue.

I jab Carlos' ribs to say
Amigo,
I know what you're thinking. If she

belonged to a different order,
wouldn't we have fun?
And if my aunt

had nuts, says Carlos,
wouldn't she more than likely be my
uncle?

Blue Rinse

In his tan washpants
and white cotton T-shirt
Carlos has the outfit to match the smile
that so often cracks
those lips above that chin. And I
would be like Carlos,
those slender legs, that torso
filled to the very edge of overflowing.
How the dark eyes lighten everything,
the dark hair tempts the nearest hand.
And clean: how he starts each day
with the mark of the woman whose face
does not reveal itself ever or at all
downtown. I have seen her
only at a distance, always both arms reaching,
one to hold, the other to attach the shirt,
the overalls, the socks, the underwear
so precisely to the clothesline.
She is a wide figure made wider

against a rising sun. And watching her
I breathe the breath of early-morning life,
blue rinse the smell, the color of the sky,
grease and guile and vinegar
all washed away like flotsam
from the fabric of a new beginning.

Schwinn

—for John Dietrich

My young son carries the fruitjar of coins
into the shop,
lifts it heavy as a sashweight
into the hands of Dietrich,
that old crippled German
who knows more about bicycles
than Carter knows about pills.

Dietrich removes the lid,
spills the coins like a miniature mountain
on the counter. What we don't tell him
is that we know to the penny
how much money the fruitjar contains:
enough to the penny to buy that
black and white Schwinn in the window.

A line forms behind us:
a young man with twisted handlebars,
a woman with a black tube around her neck
like a blowout necklace.
But Dietrich, his glasses low
on the bridge of his nose,
keeps his attention on the coins—

not from any sense of greed,
but because he takes his customers
one at a time, youngsters especially,
each step performed both
thoroughly and to perfection.

He reminds me of my German grandmother,
including the accent. Meanwhile, he

limps to the window,
takes down the bike,
presses each tire, nods, smiles,
and I think how this is the bike
I lay awake to pray for
when I was throwing the *Beacon*,
each paperbag filled to overflowing

with Goebbels and Goering and Hitler
and Tojo and Mussolini,
this is the bike that in some
inexplicable fashion
might have hastened the victory,
might have reduced somehow the pain.
Later, on the sidewalk at home,

my son will stand tall
to reach the pedals,
and I'll give him a shove
to send him handlebars and all
sparkling on a run that will come
full circle, but not quite end.
Old Dietrich seems satisfied

that the bike is ready. Perhaps
he came directly
from the old country, too,
where my grandmother lived, his hands
large like hers delivering the bike
as if the prodigy he'd stake his life on
into the hands of my suddenly older son.

Fastpitch Finals

The fireballer from downtown Omaha,
Miller Lite on his chest like an imprint,
pulls the string on a 3-2 count,
but the clean-up kid
from six miles west of Bloomfield
wrote the book on patience,

having spent most of his days
and many of his early evenings
aboard a John Deere
eating dust and making up songs
to pass the time that wasn't passing,
lyrics like *When the moon comes up*
and the stars shine bright
I'll be dancing with my steady
under blue neon light,
and tunes that he can never
remember, though he does remember
that at the moments of their improvisation
they were good, maybe damn good, maybe
even good enough to dance to,
their notes in perfect syncopation
with the popping of the tractor,

and having watched the milkcows
come to their stanchions
so deliberately in single-file,
chewing their cuds, their eyes bland,
their heavy udders swaying slowly
in a kind of massive rhythm
lightly against the insides of their thighs,

how secure in the stanchions
they slobber the grain without haste
until the grain is gone,
the grainbox then licked dark and smooth
with their long and delicate tongues,
and after the chores and the cleaning-up
and the dancing with his steady
under blue neon light
how upstairs on a thick mattress
he stretches every joint in his bone-weary body,
wanting both sleep and a re-play of the night,

so he holds back until the last instant,
then with quick lean wrists
tomahawks that floating melon
into far right center,
and before the ball touches grass
already he is rounding first,

having learned the worth
of both instant acceleration and indefinite speed
from the bully in the fourth grade
who never once caught him,
who winded to the point of collapse
would stand and try to swear,
to call him some name filthy and unforgivable,
exhaustion at last giving way to tears
while his sparse would-be victim
stood only a stone's short throw away,
silent, breathing easily, grinning,

and by the time the ball caroms off the fence
he is midway between second and third,

in his mind the bully breathing down his neck,
but he doesn't look back,

having tried that foolish trick
one Halloween around midnight,
after he and his covey of little buddies
had dumped a mean old turdhammer's outhouse,
that moment of looking back
causing him to forget the barb-wire fence,
a small scar yet on his cheek to remind him,

and when he sees the coach's right arm
spinning like the prop of a windmill
he hightails it for home,
arriving there on his belly,
yet another helping of dust
sweet as topsoil in his mouth, and
instantly he is on his feet,
brushing himself and touching his teammates' hands,
the game over and his girl
having come all that way to watch him
watching him from
high on toes
that can't stop their own mad dancing
high in the blue neon stands.

Hitting the Tree

With the meatend of my Louisville Slugger
I'm hitting the tree, a bur oak,
because my steady isn't my steady any more,
which is bad enough,
but to make things worse
she defected into the skinny arms
of Herschel Martin,
who couldn't score a run
if he hit a homer,
so I bang the tree to feel the impact
shudder bat, wrist, forearm, shoulder, spine, and
when I am recovered to the point of fresh disgust
I swing again.

In the first dream the tree will not be struck,
though I come to it enraged:
with each swing of the bat
the trunk with its roots intact
moves at the final instant just out of reach,
and I am thrown off-balance
with the force of the swing,
as if I had gone fishing
for a low outside fastball,
and composing myself I swing again,
and the tree moves again,
until fatigued and baffled and so angry now
at what I cannot reach
I almost can't remember what it was
that sent me here.

In the next the tree is a bulwark of mush,

yielding softly to each blow,
yielding as if yielding were the deepest
pleasure,
until to prevent that pleasure
I cock the bat but withhold the swing,
and the tree aches for what I'll not deliver,
it aches I tell you through the summer
and into autumn, aches into winter,
my arms raised as if the limbs
of the tree I'll not submit to,
aching.

In the last dream I am cutting down the tree.
Each time I pause to catch my breath
the wide kerf heals itself. But I am neither
discouraged nor angered. This saw is a good one,
old but sharp,
and the sawdust before each healing
drifts its ancient oakscent
like seed spilled multitudinously
onto a fertile ground. Above me,
on the highest branch,
a bird not to be identified among the leaves
sings what I take to be a song of consolation.
And when the sun goes down
I do whatever must be done
in the dark, the sawing, the resting,
the rising from the unrelenting dream.

Fishing With My Two Boys
at a Spring-Fed Pond in Kansas

Truth
like those sunfish
swimming under that overhang of willows
darts in and out among the shadows:
my boys are no longer
boys.

I sit on a campstool
trying my hand with a surface lure.
My sons meanwhile
circle the pond slowly,
looking for that perfect spot.
In their belief that such a place exists
they yet are boys, after all.
And with the luck that goes
with keeping the faith
they find it,
each landing a bass
sufficient for what lies ahead,
the multitude.

At dusk the girls, who are women,
arrive,
and by the time the first bullfrog
clears its ancient throat
we are eating the hot white flesh of the fish,
prepared and cooked by the boys
on the coals of a bonfire
tended by them,
and soon the lights in the tents

go on, then off,
and the men lie down with the women,
and their babes, who are children,
giggle until the moon drops into a cloud

and by feel I work a nightcrawler
onto a treble hook,
then spit in the general direction
of that wiggling bait,
hoping to hit it,
wanting what every lucky father wants,
more luck.

Outage

We sit suddenly in darkness
      unable to believe that
            what we cannot see

is what we're seeing, clatter
      from the television likewise
            stilled

as if a clean and consummate
      assassination. When
            I suggest The Hangout

for a cheeseburger
      and a pitcher of beer
            I am roundly applauded.

At eleven we return
      to find the outage holding.
            With a flashlight we scavenge

basement and drawer,
      one lamp and three yellow candles
            our reward. Now

in the flickering of lamp-
      light and candleflame
            we talk and talk,

measuring syllables,
      trilling phonemes. O
            how reasonable the human voice

given half a chance
      can be. And the
            aroma that rises from

wax and lampwick,
      how it brings to life those moments
            we thought so blindly

buried. When the power
      in a blink returns
            we sit silent and stunned,

seeing each other again
      in such a quaint and altogether
            different light.